PUFFIN BOOKS

Editor: Kaye Webb

A BOOK OF HEROES

'A hero has some quality that makes him what he is,' writes William Mayne, 'a quality of being slightly larger than life, and slightly larger than death too.' Here are all sorts of heroes and all kinds of heroism, gathered together from all the corners of the globe. Some of the heroes are familiar. There is Orlando, whose exploits at the Battle of Roncesvalles were sung at the Battle of Hastings in 1066. There is a fleet of sea heroes – Sir Francis Drake, Sir Richard Grenville, John Paul Jones. But there are also many less well known stories, like the one about Kâgssagssuk, the homeless Eskimo boy who became so strong that he could wring a bear's neck with his bare hands. Or the one about Völund the crippled smith tricking wicked King Nidud.

This unusual collection of tales is chosen and edited by William Mayne, who is, of course, a heroic Puffin author himself.

NB: The story of *The Minotaur* by Nathaniel Hawthorne which appears in the Hamish Hamilton hardback edition has been left out of this edition as a version of it already appears in *Tales of the Greek Heroes* by Roger Lancelyn Green.

For ages eight to twelve.

Cover design by Krystyna Turska

D1390663

A Book of

HEROES

Edited by William Mayne

Illustrated by Krystyna Turska

Penguin Books

Penguin Books Ltd, Harmondsworth, Middlesex, England
Penguin Books Inc., 7110 Ambassador Road, Baltimore, Maryland 21207, U.S.A.
Penguin Books Australia Ltd, Ringwood, Victoria, Australia

—

First published by Hamish Hamilton 1967
Published in Puffin Books 1970
Copyright © William Mayne, 1967
Illustrations copyright © Krystyna Turska, 1967

—

Made and printed in Great Britain
by Hazell Watson & Viney Ltd
Aylesbury, Bucks
Set in Monotype Bembo

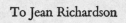
To Jean Richardson

Contents

Introduction

WHAT is a Hero? The question is not an easy one to answer always. In some of the stories that follow, the deeds of the heroes are not particularly noteworthy, and they are not always the acts of good or brave or admirable people. In fact, of some of them I would feel bound to say that you ought not to follow their examples. For instance, William of Cloudesley would not be thought an ideal Youth Club Leader. And Prince Marko was not a particularly gallant gentleman, and seemed to be a coward for most of the story.

We must conclude that heroes do not have to be good, or brave, or polite, or industrious or noble. If they are any of these things, they are them by accident.

What is a hero? It is clear that a hero has some quality that makes him what he is. I think it is a quality of being slightly larger than life (we all know people alive now who are slightly larger than life). But more than being slightly larger than life, a hero has to be slightly larger than death. Famous he may be when he lives, or even if not widely famous, well-known to some people; but it is after he is dead that the important deeds of his life seem to be done. It is in the memories of his friends, memories of what he did and what he was like, that his heroism resides. Heroes have stories told about them, they have things added to them, they become more than they were in life. They even have added to them stories that were nothing to do with them at all, tales of deeds that they did not accomplish themselves, of actions in places they never saw in ages in which they did not live. You may say that there can be very little left of a hero if he did so little that was truly his own; but I think you would be wrong. It is because of a certain quality in the living man that mere deeds and doings by lesser men were added to his score. Always the actions of men are less than the man himself. There is something about the way a thing is done that makes it a man's own. It is not always easy to say why.

There is something in the quality of his endeavour and his attitude to life that makes even the smallest of his acts memorable, and that inspires loyalty to his living presence and loyalty to his memory afterwards. And it is the most powerful character that ends up with the most heroic memory, and often with a great many tales added to him that are not heroic, particularly, but which have to be told about somebody.

There are books that are about nothing but heroes. One such book is the Mabinogion, a great cycle of Welsh stories dating from the beginning of Christian times. From this book comes the tale of Pwyll, Pryderi, and Gawl. Now, there are no great battles in the story, no huge deeds. But these people are all heroes; and if they weren't we should never have heard of them. Finn Maccumhail is another who is a hero in all he did, defeated though he is in the story told here. Sir Perceval is a hero well known throughout Europe. His most regular and notable quality is not his deeds of renown, which vary greatly, but his early upbringing, which was simple-minded rather than heroic.

But there are all sorts of heroisms here, from Drake and the great sea-fighters of five hundred years ago, to the people of the dawn of time in Finland and the Pacific, from the great beaver-haunted forests of America to the broad steppes between Russia and China, from the Bridge at Rome to the twisted labyrinth in Crete.

Pwyll, Pryderi, and Gawl

Retold by WILLIAM MAYNE

The Mabinogion, from which this story comes, is an extensive and rambling affair. It is not easy to pick out stories whole and complete, without leaving loose ends that cannot be gathered in without winding in more stories. My feeling is that the Mabinogion was related to listeners in lumps, perhaps an evening or two twice a year, like a long-drawn-out serial. There would be no difficulty in remembering where the teller had got to next time he came again, because he might be the only entertainment there had been since his last visit. This version leaves out a few small things in the middle – some adventures that Pryderi had as a boy, and the claw that came in at the window; and I have left out the whole of an Irish war, and all reference but the slightest one to Finn MacCool, who is represented elsewhere in this collection. The story as it is here is odd in shape, because the things that were begun in the first part were not brought to an end by the people in that part of the story, but by others. All the same, the story comes through quite clearly. The reason for putting it in is that everybody in the Mabinogion is a hero (or a heroine) ...

PWYLL was a Prince and a landowner, somewhere along the edge of Wales, where things are uncertain, and the enemy might be the English, or it might be Magic, or it might be your own Welsh friends, or the Irish that were your cousins over the water. At one time, in his young days, Pwyll visited one of his outlying farms, called Narberth, taking with him his bodyguard. There was a great feast got ready for him, and pigs killed, and sheep and wild birds from the hills, and the drink metheglin, as well as wine from the vineyard.

After the feast it was dark, and they sat at the fire in the hall, with the smoke sitting in the rafters, and the cup went round, and the talking with it. And the talk went the way talk often did, towards magic and ghosts and haunting and the things men had seen and not understood. The bodyguard told their tales, and Pwyll told his. Then the tenant of the farm told his. 'Just behind this house, Narberth,' he said, 'there is a mound, called Gorsedd Arberth, where there was a hero buried once, so I have heard.' But he did not know the story of that hero. 'And it is known of this mound that anyone that sits there will not come away from it without being wounded or hit, or without seeing a vision, a wonder of some sort.'

'I have heard of wonders from far away,' said Pwyll. 'But this wonder close by and on my own land is one that I shall see for myself. And if it is not a wonder but a wound or a blow, then I shall not mind that. Whoever strikes me shall be struck back in his turn, because no prince of the cantrefs of Dyved ever feared wounds or blows.'

A cantref is a hundred townships, and Pwyll was prince of seven cantrefs, or seven hundred townships. So he was not the person of least consequence in the world, and trouble would surely come on any one that hurt him.

He went out in the morning, when it had just come light, and sat on the mound called Gorsedd, and waited, ready for anything that could happen. The road through the township of Narberth ran past the mound, right to its foot and then turning away, skirting the foot of it.

In the morning light Pwyll saw something come along the road. First it was a mark, then it was a darkness, then it was a whiteness, and then it was a shining, and then it was a white horse. On the white horse was a lady with a gold garment that drew the light of the rising sun.

Pwyll was not alone, but had his guard round him, men from all over the townships and cantrefs, and even from Egypt and India and the lands beyond that. Pwyll asked them whether they knew the lady in the gold garment. The men talked to each other, but there was no one that knew her; and they told Pwyll so.

'One of you go,' said Pwyll. 'Meet her, and find who she is; because at the very least I must know who is coming through my cantrefs.' He did not say, but he knew in his heart, that the lady on the horse was the lady he wished to marry, though he had only seen her from a distance and for a moment.

One of the bodyguard jumped up and went off down the mound and on to the road, and stood waiting. But the white horse did not slow or stop. It went past like a wind, all in a flash of light, and went beyond the man.

But though the man ran as fast as he could, he did not catch it. The faster he went the further off the lady seemed to be, and though he hurried he was soon spent. He turned about and went back to Pwyll.

'Lord,' he said, 'she went so fast, like light and shade running on a hill, that I could not come near her. I think it is idle for anyone in the world to follow her on foot.' So he took a horse, and followed along the road.

But it was the same thing again. He came to a long level plain, and he could see the road going straight across it, and the white horse on the road. But the more he hurried on the further off the lady was. This time he and the horse were both spent when he turned about and came home slowly.

Pwyll was waiting for him. 'Was it no good?' said Pwyll. 'That horse you took is the fastest I have, and was it not fast enough?'

'No, Lord,' said the man. 'She went so fast, like an arrow flying down a valley, that I could not come up to her.'

'Well, she is gone now,' said Pwyll. 'I wish you could have brought her; but there is some trickery here, and perhaps she is English. But we shall go back to Narberth now.'

That night they feasted the darkness through; and early in the morning again Pwyll was on the mound Gorsedd with his men round him. This time he had his own horse ready.

'We shall not dream the same dream twice,' said the men of the bodyguard to themselves. It was not a dream, though, because in the morning light along the road there came a mark, and then a darkness, then a lightness, and then a shining, and it was the white horse.

'Give me my horse,' said Pwyll, never taking his eyes from the lady. Before he had mounted his horse she was past him, and he turned and followed, and the brass at the head of his horse sang as it swung.

His horse was fresh and ready, and he went on thinking that he would soon catch up, and that his man was wrong and had not followed with all his might.

But he came no nearer; and the faster he went the further off the lady seemed to be. So he let go of the reins and put his hands beside his mouth, to throw his voice better, and called, 'Young lady, will you wait a moment?'

The white horse stopped then, and the lady called back to Pwyll, 'Yes, I will stop.' And Pwyll came up gently to her.

'You should have asked before,' said the lady. 'Look how your horse is labouring.' But Pwyll did not hear her words, because he was looking at her face, and finding it the most beautiful he had ever seen, in his seven cantrefs or anywhere.

'Tell me,' he said, 'why do you ride through my townships and along my road in the early morning?'

'I will tell you,' said the lady. 'I rode by so that I would see you, because I have heard of you.'

'Then, here I am,' said Pwyll. 'I could not have heard better words from you. Will you tell me who you are?'

'I am Rhiannon,' said the lady. 'My father's name is Heveydd; and I have come to you for help and more than help.'

'Say what you want,' said Pwyll. 'I will gladly give it.'

'They have chosen a husband for me,' said Rhiannon, 'against my will. I have only one will in the world, and that is to declare my love to you, and I will marry no one but you, unless you reject me, and if you did that, Pwyll, then I will not care what happens to me.'

'It is strange,' said Pwyll. 'When I saw you yesterday

riding by, I knew that no other choice would I ever have but you, and if you loved me not, then I love no one.'

'Then do this for me,' said Rhiannon, 'give me your word and your pledge now, to meet me before I am given to this other man.'

'I will meet you as soon as you ask,' said Pwyll, 'wherever you wish; and the sooner and nearer the better it will be.'

'Then,' said Rhiannon, 'come to me in a year's time, a year on this day, at the palace of Heveydd my father.'

'I shall do that,' said Pwyll. 'And a short year it will be, as if I were inside the world and not on it.'

And then Rhiannon hurried on her way, going out of the plain and among the hills; and Pwyll turned back to Narberth. When they asked him how he had done, he turned the questions away and would not answer them; so that in a little while they would not ask him any more. 'No doubt,' they said, 'he has seen a wonder on the hill Gorsedd that he is not allowed to speak of.'

So Pwyll kept his peace for the rest of the year. At the end of that time he led his company towards the palace of Heveydd. Since he was a great prince, like Heveydd himself, there was great joy at this friendly visit, because in those days a visit was more likely to bring a war than a friendship. But though Pwyll brought a company with him, they were servants and notables of his own court, not an army.

Heveydd welcomed him, and all was got ready, and they had a feasting of it, and talking and drinking. Heveydd sat one side of Pwyll, and Rhiannon the other. But they were always in sight of the court, so that Pwyll could never speak to Rhiannon of the things in his heart; nor she to him. But he thought, there will be another day, when the welcoming is over, and there will be time to speak then.

The feast in the hall of Heveydd's palace was almost over, and the torches at the wall were beginning to blacken, and the wine moved slower, and the fire burnt brighter, and men began to slack their tongues and stretch at their belts, ready for the night of story-telling, when there came into the hall a red-headed tall fellow, young and of princely looks, wearing good cloth of silk. He came to Pwyll, because Pwyll was head of the table and lord of the feast, and for the day and night all visitors should come to him.

'Heaven defend you,' said Pwyll, 'and grant you plenty. Come and sit and help the night through. Bring some wine for the lord.'

'I will not sit,' said the red-headed fellow. 'I have not come to feast, but to ask you to do something for me.'

'Of course,' said Pwyll. 'Of course, I will do what you require, and listen to you.'

'Then may I say on?' said the red-headed one.

'By all means,' said Pwyll; but he should have said no more then, because the wine was at him, and at least he should have said nothing and waited until morning to counsel and grant favours. But he did not stop there. He said, 'Whatever you want, no matter what it is, I will do for you.'

'Oh,' said Rhiannon, at his side and listening. 'What are you saying, Pwyll?'

But Pwyll was foolish and smiled.

'Whatever he said,' said the red-headed one, 'he said it before all these witnesses, who are the highest of two countries, both Heveydd's and those of Dyved, and can he not be held to it?'

'It is true,' said Rhiannon.

'It is true,' said Pwyll. 'But say on, lad.'

'You have come here to marry a lady,' said the red-headed one. 'And that lady is beside you now, Rhiannon. I have come tonight to ask you to give her up to me, and to give up to me also the feast that you are lord of, so that it can be my own wedding feast.'

Then Pwyll's wits cleared, and he knew that he had spoken with an addled brain, and that silence would have been better. But there was nothing for him to say.

'It is useless to sulk,' said Rhiannon. 'That brings no man

out of his folly. What wits you have you have used badly tonight, Pwyll.'

'But lady,' said Pwyll, 'who would have thought such a question could come? Who would have known such a demand was possible? In truth, I took him for someone of noble kind, who would not ask a thing like that.'

'This is Gawl, the son of Clud,' said Rhiannon. 'It is to him that they would marry me, against my will. But now you too have spoken against me, and I shall have to go to him.'

'I will go back on my word,' said Pwyll. 'And I would get up and fight now, before the court's assembly; but the wine is in my knees and I cannot stand. I can only talk.'

'You had best be silent,' said Rhiannon. 'But listen, if your ears are not dizzy. First, you have promised me to him, and second, he is Gawl, son of Clud, and Clud is a great and wealthy king, of great power. So for two reasons you must do as he asked. One is that your honour demands that you do what your tongue promised, and the other is that if you do not there will be a defeat on you from the men of Clud; and there is shame either way. So give me to Gawl, willingly, and I promise you that I will never be his bride.'

Pwyll wondered and thought, and could not understand how anything could come right; but he did what Rhiannon told him, and she said what she had in her mind, and they talked together for a long time.

Gawl sat and drank and waited. Then he stood and said, 'Lord, I have waited a long time now. How is your word and your promise?'

'My promise was given,' said Pwyll. 'And what I can give you I will give you. That is, you shall have Rhiannon to be your wife.'

'But as for the other,' said Rhiannon, 'that is, the lordship of the feast, that is not Pwyll's to give, because it was given to him by my house, and I gave it not only to him but to all his people, and his household and the warriors that are here. And

I cannot take it away. And there is no more after this, as you know, Gawl: this is the year's feast. But you shall come back in a year from now, and take the head of the table, and have your men about you, and that night I shall become your bride, as Pwyll has promised.'

'Then I shall come again in a year,' said Gawl, and he set down his wine cup and went away from the hall.

So another year went by, and Pwyll and Gawl each had something to wait for. At the end of the time Gawl came back to the palace of Heveydd, to the feast that was made ready for him, because that was what was promised. Pwyll came too, with a hundred of his bodyguard. But he was not dressed in silk like Gawl, and he was not received gladly, like Gawl. Instead he was dressed in rags and cast clouts and wore Irish boots of wood on his feet, instead of fine English shoes.

Gawl was brought to the head of the feast, and Pwyll stayed outside, dressed as he was like a beggar. But when the eating was over, and the long night of drinking was to begin, Pwyll went into the hall, because it was the custom that poor people could enter after the meat and take what was given from the broken pieces.

Pwyll came up to Gawl, at the head of the table, and said: 'I greet you, Lord, and all your company, and Heaven bless you, and reward you.'

'May Heaven prosper you too,' said Gawl, 'and my own greeting to you as well.'

'Then,' said Pwyll, 'I have something to ask you, if you will be good enough to grant my wish.'

'Ask your favour,' said Gawl, 'and if it is reasonable, then I will grant it.'

'It is reasonable, I hope,' said Pwyll; and no one knew who he was, in his rags and tatters. 'I am hungry, and my family too, waiting for me in another place. All I ask is to fill this small bag full of broken meats from the feast table, whatever can be spared.'

It was a usual request, because it was not the custom for beggars to take away the bounty they were offered without asking it.

'You are welcome to that,' said Gawl, because the bag was not very big. 'Bring him food.'

And food was brought, first by one attendant, and then by two, and then by four. But however much they brought, the bag became no fuller. It swallowed all that was put into it.

'Oh, king of beggars,' said Gawl, 'that is a wonderful bag. Will it ever be full?'

'No,' said Pwyll. 'It can never be full and carried away unless a great lord, possessing lands and domains and castles and treasure, and in the line of kings, shall come and tread down with both his feet the food that is inside, and say that enough has been put in. And I beg you will do it, Lord, because there is so much in already that I shall not be able to carry it.'

Then Rhiannon spoke. 'Do it for him, Gawl,' she said. 'And then we can send him away, no doubt.'

'I will,' said Gawl. He got up from his place at the feast and put both feet in the bag, and began to tread down the food that was in it. And Pwyll lifted up the sides of the bag, so that they went above Gawl's head, closed it over him, and pulled the slipthongs tight, and tied a knot. Then he blew the horn that was at his waist.

At once his own knights came into the palace, and overcame all the men that came with Gawl, who had eaten well and begun to drink well too, and put them in the prison of the castle. Pwyll threw off his rags and his Irish boots and his tattered hat. And as they came in, each one of Pwyll's men struck a blow on the bag, and asked: 'What is in here?'

Each man said it was a badger, and a badger was called an evil reptile in those days, so that blows and kicks were all that Gawl had, inside the bag.

Then all the knights had gone by, and Gawl spoke. 'Lord,' he said, 'I do not know who you are, but you have worked a trick upon me, and overcome me. But I do not think it worthy that I should be killed in a bag.'

'That is true,' said Pwyll, 'and I will not kill you in a bag. But I will consider what I shall do.'

'My soul,' said Rhiannon to Pwyll. 'There are things to be considered. Do not take his life. Instead, make him pay for the feast that we have had, because there are the minstrels and the beggars and the serving people to satisfy. Then make him promise to take no revenge on us for what we have done to him, and that will be enough.'

Gawl heard what was said, and he agreed; and Pwyll agreed too. So they came to an arrangement, and Gawl came from the bag, very much bruised and hurt, and went to his own lands, leaving his own men to do all that had to be done.

Then the feast went on that had been interrupted, and the drinking and the singing and the tales went on all night, and at the end of it Pwyll and Rhiannon were married. And the next day they went out towards Pwyll's own land, the land of Dyved and the seven cantrefs, where there was yet more feasting and bringing of gifts and giving of gifts. And Gawl was silent for the rest of their lives.

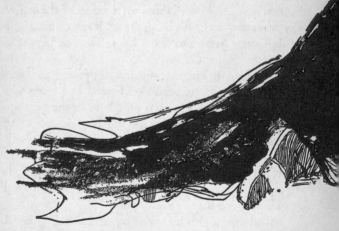

But Gawl took his revenge, and kept his promise too, and it was like this. Pwyll and Rhiannon had a son, and they named him Pryderi. When Pryderi was grown, his father died; and Pryderi married Kicva, the daugher of Gwynn Gloy.

Now Pryderi, when he was a lad, had been out in the courts of other rulers, because that was the way of young princes in those days; and he had a friend who was older than he, whose name was Manawyddan, the son of King Llyr, who is sometimes called Lear. Now, Manawyddan had been at a war in Ireland, and when he came back he found that he was homeless, because what he had had been taken by his cousin.

'Sadness upon me,' he said. 'And misery. I have nowhere to lay my head. My cousin has taken all, and will not let me have it back.'

'Now,' said Pryderi, 'you were never a man with any land or possessions, and you can live in your cousin's palace, as you did before when that giant of a man that frightened the Irish, Bendigeid Vran, was ruler.'

'I cannot be happy with him,' said Manawyddan. 'Not with my cousin. What is he? What is he in comparison with my brother the giant, my brother Bendigeid Vran that is now dead? What shall I do, Pryderi?'

'You are a simple fellow,' said Pryderi. 'But good. Will you listen to what I have to say?'

'I will,' said Manawyddan; and since they were at that time in a grassy place, they lay down and talked.

'Seven cantrefs belong to me,' said Pryderi, 'and my mother lives in them. Now it seems right to me that I should give these seven cantrefs and seven hundred townships to her, and when I have done that, then I will give her and the cantrefs to you, and if you marry her, and have these seven cantrefs, you will not find a better lady, nor fairer lands in the whole of Wales. For I have other lands that came to me with Kicva that was the daughter of Gwynn Gloy.'

'To a man that only needed advice you are giving a world,' said Manawyddan. 'To a man that only asked for a piece of the world you are giving Heaven. I will not waste time on yes. I will not waste time on no. I shall go now and find Rhiannon, and look at your cantrefs.'

'Go then,' said Pryderi, 'and for all your long speech you are still a simple good fellow that I love. Yet remember that I can promise Rhiannon, but not Rhiannon's love, which is hers alone.'

They set out together, and came in the end to Dyved. A feast was made for them at once, because Manawyddan was a guest, and Pryderi was the lord. But Manawyddan said nothing to Rhiannon of what Pryderi had said, and Pryderi said nothing either, so that Rhiannon could feel love first. So Manawyddan and Rhiannon sat next to each other at the feast, and Manawyddan looked at Rhiannon, and his heart warmed to her, and he saw that the years of life had not taken away but added grace and beauty, so that she was filled with them. And Rhiannon was glad to speak to this simple and gentle big man. He was no giant, though, like his dead brother Bendigeid Vran.

'Pryderi,' said Manawyddan, when the feast was well on, and the carousal had to begin, the drinking to dawn, 'I am glad that I came with you, and I would be glad if you will do as you promised, and make good your saying.'

'What saying was that?' said Rhiannon.

'It was this,' said Pryderi. 'That I would give you the seven cantrefs I had from Pwyll my father, and that I would give you to my friend Manawyddan to be his wife.'

Then Rhiannon thought for a space, while the feasting of the men and retainers went on round her. Then she said: 'I will do it gladly.'

'And so will I,' said Manawyddan. 'It may be that I have little, and no lands, but what I have is yours.'

Then, in the fashion of those days, they were married during the feast, and she became his bride.

And after that the four of them, Pryderi and Kicva, Manawyddan and Rhiannon, lived happily in Dyved, in the seven cantrefs, where they hunted and took their pleasure; because there were no better lands to live in, nor more pleasant, nor better hunting grounds, nor greater plenty of honey and fish. And they all loved one another greatly, and were never parted from each other.

Then they came to Narberth, in the round that they made, and were feasted there. Then, after the feast, when tales were told again of the mound behind Narberth, they left the hall and went up there, to Gorsedd, to see what fortunes did for them, because they were not afraid of blows and hurts or of visions and wonders.

And as they sat in the light of early morning there came a great peal of thunder that rang out round the mound and round the country. And straight after the lightning there was a fall of mist, so thick that they could not see one another, only hear the moving. After the mist it became light all round again, like another day; and indeed it was another day, because when they looked down towards Narberth and the farmyard that was behind the hall, there was nothing there but the walls of the hall itself. There were no cattle, there were no horses, no smoke, no fire, no men, no huts, no bodyguard, and within the fences there was no growing thing but weeds of the wilderness. And wherever they looked they saw they were alone, and they did not know what had happened.

They went down to Narberth, and into the hall. There was no man to greet them or stay them, in sleeping place or cellar or kitchen; but it was all laid in ruin. So they left that place, and began to go through the land, and all the possessions of Dyved. They found nothing but wild beasts; there was nothing there that had been led by man's hand. So, when they had finished what they carried with them, they ate what they killed in hunting, because their horses and their dogs were all they had.

One morning Pryderi and Manawyddan went to hunt, and

set the dogs off before to find and follow. And the dogs soon
set something, behind a bush, and went to bring it out and
tear it down. But the dogs turned away in fear, and came back
to the men, with their hair bristled up greatly.

'Now,' said Pryderi, 'here is game worth having, if the
dogs will not lay hold of it. Let us go and see.'

So they went to the bush, and when they got to it a wild
boar of a pure white got up from behind it where he had been
lying. The men set the dogs on again, and the boar moved
away a little; but the dogs would not touch him.

Then the boar ran away, and the dogs after, and Pryderi
and Manawyddan went up a nearby mound, that was
Gorsedd, to watch and see where they went, because the dogs
would bring back the boar to be killed. And the men watched
the chase.

Then they suddenly saw that there was a castle built in
a place where nothing had ever been before, not even a
stone. But now there was a new building, freshly made,
and high. And the boar ran into it, and the dogs ran after
him.

'It is all wonders,' said Pryderi. 'What is this building?'

'Whatever it is, I do not like it, not very well,' said Manawyddan. 'No, not at all.'

'Let us wait for the dogs,' said Pryderi. So they stood on
Gorsedd and waited for the dogs. But they heard nothing of
the dogs, and saw nothing, and there was perfect silence all
round them.

'I must go for the dogs,' said Pryderi, when they had waited
a long time. 'I will go peaceably and ask at the castle.'

'I do not like it,' said Manawyddan. 'I do not think it
would be wise to go into the castle, because we have never
seen it until this moment. You know there is a spell on this
land; and whoever put the spell on it has put the castle here
also.'

'It may be so,' said Pryderi. 'But I will not give up my dogs
for magic.' And he would not listen to Manawyddan and

left him standing uneasily on the hill, and went down to the castle.

The castle was like the rest of the land. It was deserted, neither man nor beast being in it. And no boar either, and no dogs.

But in the middle of the floor he came upon a marble fountain, standing white in the sunlight, and on the edge of the fountain a golden bowl, like sunlight itself, and the bowl hung from golden chains, and the chains grew from the air and there was no top to the chains. They appeared from the upper air and hung from a clear sky.

Pryderi stopped to look upon this wonder of a fountain, and at the work of the bowl. Then he touched the bowl with both hands to pick it up. And when he did his hands stuck to it, and his feet stuck to the marble slabs of the fountain, and sadness came on his soul, and his tongue was not able to move. And so he stood.

Manawyddan waited for him long times, until the end of the day. Then, late in the evening, when he was sure that Pryderi and the dogs must be dead for ever, and he would never hear of them again, he went back to Rhiannon and Kicva.

'Where is Pryderi?' said Rhiannon, 'Pryderi and the dogs?'

'I will tell you all I know,' said Manawyddan; and he sat heavy with sadness at the feet of Rhiannon and Kicva and told them all that he knew.

Then, 'Let this be between us,' said Rhiannon, 'that you were not the best companion for Pryderi.'

'And between me and thee too,' said Kicva, 'that you have lost for us a better man than was left.'

Then Rhiannon got up from her place, and walked off into the waste lands, towards the place where the castle had sprung up. And when she came to the place she went in, and saw Pryderi holding the bowl, and the bowl holding him, and the marble holding him too. And she took hold of the bowl with him, and was fastened to it, and to the ground, as he was. And then it became night, and a fall of mist came, and the castle vanished, and Pryderi and Rhiannon with it.

Then Manawyddan and Kicva were full of sorrow; and they were hungry too, because they had nothing that day, and they had no dogs to catch them more. So they left the cantrefs of Dyved, and went into England, as poor souls.

Manawyddan took up a craft that he knew of. He became a maker of shoes, though it was sad work for a prince. But it was all he knew. And he and Kicva lived in England and made shoes, and sold them, and lived on the money, and saved some. And what they saved they laid out in wheat; so that after a time they came back to Dyved, and Narberth, and ploughed out the wild fields, and sowed three of them with wheat, three crofts of it. And it was summer, and he hunted and caught fish, and kept himself and Kicva.

Then it came to harvest time. Manawyddan looked at the first croft of wheat, and it was nearly ready. He said: 'I will take the sickle to it tomorrow,' and he went to Narberth to wait the night. But when he went out in the dawn to cut when the stalks were soft, he found nothing but the bare standing straw. Every ear of wheat had been cut away and taken, so that there was no crop for him.

There was nothing he could do to remedy it. He went to the second croft, and saw that was ready to be cut the next day. And he went to Narberth and waited the night. But when he came in the early morning he found nothing but the bare straw. 'Oh Heaven,' he said. 'I know that whatever is trying to ruin us and all our land is now finishing his task; and we shall be for ever taken away from the land we love.'

He went to the third croft, and looked at that, and it was ready as the others had been, and ripe for cutting the next day. And Manawyddan went towards Narberth. But he did not wait there. He came back before darkness was over the land, and he laid down to wait, saying to himself that he would see what it was that spoiled all the work and stole the grain.

At midnight he heard something in the wheat; and he looked; but at first he could see nothing. Then he saw it was a mighty numerous host of mice that swarmed on the wheat, and bit off the heads and carried them away, by climbing the straw and bending it over with their weight, until it lay close to the ground, and then biting it off. And each straw had a mouse, so many they were.

Manawyddan rushed on the mice; but they were so many, and though he was the brother of a giant, not one did he catch, because they all fled away with their burden. There was only one, and she went slowly, and he caught her and put her in his glove, and went back to Narberth.

'What have you there?' said Kicva, when she saw Manawyddan put his glove by the string on a peg.

'A thief,' said Manawyddan, 'that I found robbing me;' and Kicva laughed. But he told her what he had seen. 'And tomorrow,' he said, 'I will hang the thief in a gallows.'

'That is worthy work indeed for a prince,' said Kicva, 'to hang a mouse. Manawyddan, do you not know that it is unseemly for a man of dignity like yourself to touch a reptile like a mouse?'

'I would hang them all, if I could catch them,' said Manawyddan. 'What else would you have me do?'

'I will not help the mouse,' said Kicva, 'except to bring shame away from you. So do as you think right, Lord.'

In the morning Manawyddan went to the mound Gorsedd, with the mouse. And he set up a little gallows on the mound. And while he was doing this, there came a traveller towards him, a wise man, a scholar, such as used to wander in Dyved before the trouble came to the land, fully seven years. And he was the first man that Manawyddan had seen in Dyved in all that time.

'What are you doing?' said the scholar.

'I am hanging a thief,' said Manawyddan. 'And that is my right and my duty.'

'But what a thief,' said the scholar. 'I see it in your hand like a mouse. Surely such a thief can do so little ill that it is not worth hanging. Let it go free, Lord.'

'Never,' said Manawyddan.

'Oh come,' said the scholar. 'I will give you a pound to let it free.'

'I will not let it free, nor will I sell it,' said Manawyddan.

And at that the scholar went on his way.

And when he had gone, and Manawyddan was putting a cross-bar to the gallows, there came a priest, with the same question: 'What are you doing, Lord?'

And Manawyddan had the same answer: 'Hanging a thief.'

'Such a nobleman should not touch such a reptile,' said the priest. 'I will give you three pounds to let it go.'

'I will not take any price for it,' said Manawyddan. And the priest went on his way.

And Manawyddan put the noose round the neck of the mouse, and he was about to draw it up, when there came a bishop, and all his retinue and singing boys.

And the bishop himself walked to Manawyddan.

'My lord,' said Manawyddan. 'I may ask thy blessing on a good work.'

'Be blessed indeed,' said the bishop, 'but what is this good work?'

'Hanging a thief,' said Manawyddan.

'I see only a mouse,' said the bishop. 'I will give you seven pounds for it, now that I have come at the doom of the reptile. Seven pounds; and I have it in gold.'

'It is ready to hang, and hanged it will be,' said Manawyddan. 'Watch, my lord.'

'Stay,' said the bishop. 'I will give twenty-four pounds to you to set the reptile free.'

'No, never,' said Manawyddan.

'I will give you all the horses with their loads in my company,' said the bishop, 'which is all minster gold.'

'No, indeed,' said Manawyddan. 'And I had thy blessing first, and I will do my hanging at last.'

'Stay again,' said the bishop. 'What will you have?'

'I will have Pryderi and Rhiannon,' said Manawyddan.

'That you shall have,' said the bishop. 'Now let go the reptile.'

'Not yet,' said Manawyddan. 'Next the spell must be taken off Dyved and the seven cantrefs, so that there is no more charm and illusion.'

'That too you will have,' said the bishop. 'Now let it go.'

'No,' said Manawyddan. 'Unless you tell me who this reptile is, that so many should come with such store to ransom her.'

'She is my wife,' said the bishop; but he appeared as a bishop no more. 'I am Lloyd, the son of Kilwed, and I cast the charm over the seven cantrefs of Dyved, to avenge Gawl, the son of Clud, that had dishonour from Pwyll, the father of Pryderi, to be a vengeance for the beating in the bag that Pwyll played upon him. And when you came back into the land with your wheat, all my household changed themselves to mice, and came to spoil the crop; and my wife among them. And it is only that she has a child soon to be born that she ran slowly and you caught her. But I will change her for whatever you wish. And now I shall vanish, and Pryderi and Rhiannon shall be with you when I go, and all the charm and illusion shall be lifted from the land.'

And so it was. Pryderi and Rhiannon came across the mound Gorsedd, and the mouse dropped from Manawyddan's hand, and changed to a young woman, and went with the bishop.

And they looked round the land in the morning light, and they saw that it was tilled and peopled and full of stock, as it had been before the seven years began.

And once more they lived with great happiness in the seven cantrefs of Dyved, and took their pleasure, and were blessed.

How Finn Maccumhail was in the House of the Rowan Tree without Power to Stand or Leave to Sit Down

ALAN GARNER

Don't worry about how to pronounce Finn Maccumhail. Just say Fin Macool and you are right. In extreme cases say Fingal, and you are just as right. It is the same person, in different parts of the land: Ireland and Scotland and the Isle of Man. Finn is the leader of a band of warriors, and a great deal of telling of the story was done, so that a great deal was added to the legend as time went on; and there was adventure after adventure. He himself probably lived in about A.D. 250, and was most likely a general employed by the King of Tara to conquer the rest of Ireland. Finn and his company, who are all well-marked characters, wander about Ireland, not seeming to have much to do most of the time, but having to fight now and then to defend Ireland (as, for instance, against the Welsh in the piece I have left out of the middle of the story of Pwyll and Pryderi). You will find all the characters in all the stories distinct and humorous – they were remembered by the story-tellers as people, not as personalities – and I find that though Finn Maccumhail is not my favourite hero, some of the stories about him are my favourite hero stories. The author of this version points out that there are many ways of telling this story, and his favourite one is that of Alexander Cameron, roadman between Duror and Ballachulish, whose version he has followed, with strands from the best of the others.

A DAY Finn and his men were on the hunting hill they stopped in a place behind the wind and at the face of the sun, where they could see everyone and no one at all could see them.

There came the blackness of a shower from the east, and in

it a Wandering Big Lad. Finn greeted him and asked where he
was from and what was the juice of his coming.

'I have travelled through night-watching and sea storm,'
said the Big Lad, 'to be with you, and the juice of my coming
is to lay on you, Finn Maccumhail, as crosses and spells and
seven fairy fetters of going and straying, that you shall be my
guest in the House of the Rowan Tree; and the earth shall
make a hollow in your foot and the sky a nest in the crown of
your head before you turn from this journey.'

'Up and down with your crosses and spells!' said Finn.

'Neither up nor down,' said the Big Lad, and he showed
the back of his head to them and went.

'That head,' said Conan, 'would be as low as his heels,
were I asked.'

'You are not asked,' said Finn.

'There is no luck in Wandering Lads,' said Conan.

'Conan, you never see a man frown but you would strike
him, and for that many are headless today who have blinked
at hearth-smoke.'

Finn set his boat to the waves, and raced as kilns of fire over
the red divisions of the universe to find the Big Lad at the
House of the Rowan Tree.

'Conan,' said Finn at the end of a day and a year, 'what do
you see?'

'If it is a crow,' said Conan from the mast, 'it is big. But if
it is land, it is small.'

They were not long in coming to it, and they drew the ship
up her own measure nine times on grey grass, so that the
scholars of a grand town could not laugh at her, and went on
themselves till they met with the Big Lad at the House of the
Rowan Tree.

The Big Lad greeted them with words and asked them to
go in with him to eat. They did so, and Finn marvelled at the
richness of the place, for the walls were lined with boards of
many colours, blue, white, black, green and red; and the
seats and the floor were covered with gold-embroidered cloth;

and there were gowns of silk laid ready for the guests; and the air was full of perfume that refreshed the hearts of those that breathed it.

The Big Lad told Finn to range himself and his men for feasting, and then he left them. Conan threw his length down by the fire, and the rest were settled along the walls.

'I think it a wonder,' said Finn after a while, 'that the feast is not coming.'

'I think it a greater wonder,' said Goll MacMorna, 'that the sweet smell has become a midden.'

'And a greater wonder yet,' said Glas, 'is the painted wall that is now bare wattle.'

'Even greater the wonder,' said Faolan, 'that the many doors to the place are now only one, and that as narrow and low as a sty.'

'The greatest wonder,' said Conan, 'is that not a thread of silk gown nor of embroidered gold is left, and I cannot move from here, but there is the feel of clay about me close, as cold as the snow of a night.'

Then Finn and his men would have armed themselves against attack, but whatever part of them touched the House of the Rowan Tree stuck fast, and Conan on the floor could not even turn his head, but lay in a pool of thatch drip.

'Put your thumb to your knowledge teeth,' said Goll to Finn, 'and see what can save us from this trap.'

'Nothing,' said Finn, 'will loose us from the place where we are but the blood of the three sons of the King of Insh Tilly strained through silver rings into cups of gold.'

Conan shouted from the hearthstone, 'And did I not tell you in good time what would happen to you with your Wandering Lads?'

Finn did not answer, but remembered that Oscar and Lohary had not been with him that day when they were at the hunting hill and the Big Lad had brought them to this death-strait. So he lifted his head and gave his war cry, the Dord-Fiann, and the sound of it would pass through the borders of the world and the time to come, and he knew that when Oscar and Lohary would hear the sound they would speed to him from any quarter in which they might be. And before a sun rose next day Oscar and Lohary were crying outside the wall, 'Are you there, Finn? What have we to do now?'

Finn told them not to touch the house, and that nothing would release him from it but the blood of the three sons of

the King of Insh Tilly strained through silver rings into cups of gold.

'Where shall we watch for these three sons?' said Oscar.

'Watch well the ford mouth between the night and the day,' said Finn. 'A great host will be there with them.'

'Then how shall we know them?' said Lohary.

'They will walk apart from the host on the right hand, and have on them green garments.'

Oscar and Lohary went away to find the rings and cups for
straining and holding the blood. At the feel of night they heard
a loud coming.

Lohary said, 'We shall go out of the water and meet them
on the land.' And so they did.

When the great host was near it cried, 'Who are those two
standing at the mouth of ford and night? Whoever they are it
is time for them to be afraid.'

'A third of your fear be on yourselves, and a small third of
it be on us,' said Oscar.

Then they met, but Oscar and Lohary let none escape from
the edge of their weapons but one person, to say what had
become of the rest.

Next morning they told Finn how it was, but that they
saw no King's sons.

'Watch well the ford mouth of the river tonight,' said
Finn.

It was a great host that came against Oscar and Lohary that
night. 'Who are these?' they said. 'It is time for them to be
afraid.'

'Two thirds of your fear be on yourselves,' answered
Lohary, 'and a little third of it be on us.'

Oscar and Lohary stood the ford, and let none escape from
the edge of their weapons but one person, to say what had
become of the rest.

'And the King's children did not come that night yet,' said
Oscar to Finn. And as soon as the greying of the evening was
on them Finn said, 'Let your rings and cups be with you
tonight.'

Then the heroes went away to the ford mouth of the
river, and advanced across to the dry land. They were a
short time waiting when they saw a great host coming towards them, and on the right hand the three sons of the
King of Insh Tilly, wearing green garments.

'Will you face the three sons of the King of Insh Tilly or
the great host?' said Oscar.

Lohary said, 'I will face the three sons of the King of Insh Tilly, and you shall face the great host.'

The host cried, 'Who are these standing above the ford mouth of the river in the evening? Whoever they are it is time for them to flee tonight.'

'Three thirds of your fear be on yourselves,' said Oscar, 'and none at all of it on us.'

Then Oscar met the great host, and Lohary the three sons of the King.

There was a fight between Oscar and the host, but he left not the one of them alive, for he was in haste to be where Lohary was. Lohary had the three sons on their knees, and when Oscar saw this it was not on helping Lohary he was active, but on the blood, for it was pouring out on the meadow.

He began to strain it through silver rings into cups of gold, but before all the cups were full the bodies were so stiff that out of them more would not flow.

'We have come,' said Oscar, 'having the blood with us.'

'Well,' said Finn, 'rub it to every bit of you that may touch the house.' They did that, and went in. They began to release the men by rubbing blood to every bit of them where they touched the house, and every man was free but Conan.

For him there was left only the stain on the cups. The hair and skin stuck to the hearthstone and they had to leave him bound as he was. 'If I had been a young girl,' Conan shouted after them, 'you would not have left me to the last.'

Finn and his men went home, but they had not gone far when they looked back and saw Conan coming forward. There he was, neither a thread of hair nor a strip of skin between the top of his head and his heels, and from that day he was named Bald Conan.

That was the worst death-strait in which Finn ever was, when he was in the House of the Rowan Tree, without power to stand or leave to sit down.

Hynd Horn

ANONYMOUS

Hind Horn he is called sometimes, and other times Prince Horn, and the story has been recounted many times. This ballad version has the bones of it; though it is not the most heroic Horn who appears here. I don't think romantic heroes are the heroes for this book; but that is what Horn looks like being here. Yet he isn't a mere romantic hero, but something more solid. In other versions of the tale he is a fighting man, leading a band of mad Irishmen, who overcome the king that has stolen the princess away. In this version the girl is called Jean, but usually she is Rymenhild; and the king he has to fight is the Saracen King of Suddene. It is probably not possible to say very often which is the proper and pure version, or which is the best version, or which is the most perfect version of any story that has come down with so many strands. The truth is that there was a hero, and things began to stick to him; not only what he had done, but what other people had done; so that in the end, in the north country there might be one version, and in the west another that was all opposed and contradictory. Here is one edition of the Horn story. If you have others don't throw any of them away, but keep them as a collection: you may get more.

> Hynd Horn's bound, love, and Hynd Horn's free,
> With a hey lillelu and a how lo lan;
> Where was ye born, or in what countrie?
> And the birk and the broom blows bonnie.
>
> 'In good greenwood, there I was born,
> And all my forebears me beforn.
>
> 'O seven long years I served the King,
> And as for wages I never got none;
>
> 'But ae sight of his ae daughter,
> And that was thro' an auger-bore.'

Seven long years he served the King,
And it's all for the sake of his daughter, Jean.

The King an angry man was he;
He sent young Hynd Horn to the sea.

He's given his love a silver wand
With seven silver laverocks sittin' thereon.

She's given to him a gay gold ring
With seven bright diamonds set therein.

'As long's these diamonds keep their hue,
Ye'll know I am a lover true.

'But when the ring turns pale and wan,
Ye may ken that I love anither man.'

He hoist up sails and away sail'd he
Till that he came to a foreign countrie.

One day as he look'd his ring upon,
He saw the diamonds pale and wan.

He's left the seas and he's come to the land,
And the first that he met was an old beggar man.

'What news, what news? thou old beggar man,
For it's seven years sin I've seen land.'

'No news,' said the beggar, 'no news at all,
But there is a wedding in the King's hall.

'But there is a wedding in the King's ha'
That has halden these forty days and twa'.'—

'Cast off, cast off thy old beggar weed,
And I'll give thee my good grey steed:

'And lend to me your wig of hair
To cover mine, because it is fair.'—

'My begging weed is not for thee,
Your riding steed is not for me.'

But part by right and part by wrong
Hynd Horn has changed with the beggar man.

The old beggar man was bound for to ride
But young Hynd Horn was bound for the bride.

When he came to the King's gate,
He sought a drink for Hynd Horn's sake.

The bride came tripping down the stair,
With the scales of red gold in her hair.

With a cup of red wine in her hand,
And that she gave to the old beggar man.

Out of the cup he drank the wine,
And into the cup he dropt the ring.

'O, got ye this by sea or land?
Or got ye it off a dead man's hand?'—

'I got it not by sea nor land,
But I got it, madam, off your own hand.'

'O, I'll cast off my gowns of brown,
And beg with you from town to town.

'O, I'll cast off my gowns o' red,
And I'll beg with you to win my bread.

'O, I'll take the scales of gold from my hair,
And I'll follow you for evermair.'

She hast cast away the brown and the red,
And she's follow'd him to beg her bread.

She has taken the scales of gold from her hair
And she's follow'd him for evermair.

But between the kitchen and the hall
He has let his cloutie cloak down fall.

And the red gold shined over him a',
With a hey lillelu, and a how lo lan;
And the bride from the bridegroom was town awa'
And the birk and the broom blows bonnie.

Kâgssagssuk, the Homeless Boy who became a Strong Man

Edited and translated by W. WORSTER

This story was told by Polar Eskimos of South Sound, somewhere north and west of Greenland. The Eskimos are not a nation but a race, and though they look alike to the eye of memory, there are differences between tribes under the fur coats. In their stories there is no mention of kings and queens. The highest among them is the wizard, and the most noble the strong man, and their wealth is in their skill in fishing and sealing and using the kayak and the umiak. The animal they keep is the dog, and they do not keep him as a pet or even as a watchdog, but as a puller of sledges. Kâgssagssuk is a hero, of the sort that rises from misfortune to great power through deeds slightly larger than life.

ONE day, it is said, when the men and women in the place had gone to a spirit calling, the children were left behind, all in one big house, where they played, making a great noise.

A homeless boy named Kâgssagssuk was walking about alone outside, and it is said that he called to those who were playing inside the house, and said:

'You must not make so much noise, or the Great Fire will come.'

The children, who would not believe him, went on with their noisy play, and at last the Great Fire appeared. Little Kâgssagssuk fled into the house, and cried:

'Lift me up. I must have my gloves, and they are up there!'

So they lifted him up to the drying frame under the roof.

And then they heard the Great Fire come hurrying into the house from without. He had a great live ribbon seal for a whip, and that whip had long claws. And then he began dragging the children out through the passage with his great whip, and each time he drew one out, that one was frizzled up. And at last there were no more. But before going away, the Great Fire reached up and touched with his finger a skin which was hanging on the drying frame.

As soon as the Great Fire had gone away, little Kâgssagssuk crawled down from the drying frame and went over to the people who were gathered in the wizard's house, and told them what had happened. But none believed what he said.

'You have killed them yourself,' they declared.

'Very well, then,' said he, 'if you think so, try to make a noise yourselves, like the children did.'

And now they began cooking blubber above the entrance to the house, and when the oil was boiling and bubbling as hard as it could, they began making a mighty noise. And true enough, up came the Great Fire outside.

But little Kâgssagssuk was not allowed to come into the house, and therefore he hid himself in the store shed. The Great Fire came into the house, and brought with it the live ribbon seal for a whip. They heard it coming in through the passage, and then they poured boiling oil over it, and his whip being thus destroyed, the Great Fire went away.

But from that time onward, all the people of the village were unkind to little Kâgssagssuk, and that although he had told the truth. Up to that time he had lived in the house of Umerdlugtoq, who was a great man, but now he was forced to stay outside always, and they would not let him come in. If he ventured to step in, though it were for no more than to dry his boots, Umerdlugtoq, that great man, would lift him up by the nostrils, and cast him over the high threshold again.

And little Kâgssagssuk had two grandmothers; the one of these beat him as often as she could, even if he only lay out in the passage. But his other grandmother took pity on him, because he was the son of her daughter, who had been a

woman like herself, and therefore she dried his clothes for
him.

When, once in a while, that unfortunate boy did come in,
Umerdlugtoq's folk would give him some tough walrus
hide to eat, wishing only to give him something which they
knew was too tough for him. And when they did so, he
would take a little piece of stone and put it between his teeth,
to help him, and when he had finished, put it back in his
breeches, where he always kept it. When he was hungry, he
would sometimes eat of the dogs' leavings on the ground
outside, finding there walrus hide which even the dogs refused to eat.

He slept among the dogs, and warmed himself up on the
roof, in the warm air from the smoke hole. But whenever
Umerdlugtoq saw him warming himself there, he would haul
him down by the nostrils.

Thus a long time passed, and it had been dark in the winter,
and was beginning to grow light near the coming of spring.
And now little Kâgssagssuk began to go wandering about the
country. Once when he was out, he met a big man, a giant,
who was cutting up his catch, and on seeing him, Kâgssagssuk
cried out in a loud voice:

'Ho, you man there, give me a piece of that meat!'

But although he shouted as loudly as he could, that giant
could not hear him. At last a little sound reached the big
man's ears, and then he said:

'Bring me luck, bring me luck!'

And he threw down a little piece of meat on the ground,
believing it was one of the dead who thus asked.

But little Kâgssagssuk, who, young as he was, had already
some helping spirits, made that little piece of meat to be a
big piece, just as the dead can do, and ate as much as he could,
and when he could eat no more, there was still so much left
that he could hardly drag it away to hide it.

Some time after this, little Kâgssagssuk said to his mother's
mother:

'I have by chance become possessed of much meat, and my thoughts will not leave it. I will therefore go out and look at it.'

So he went off to the place where he had hidden it, and it was not there. And he fell to weeping, and while he stood there weeping, the giant came up.

'What are you weeping for?'

'I cannot find the meat which I had hidden in a store-place here.'

'Ho,' said the giant, 'I took the meat. I thought it had belonged to another one.'

And then he said again: 'Now let us play together.' For he felt kindly towards that boy, and had pity on him.

And they two went off together. When they came to a big stone, the giant said: 'Now let us push this stone.' And they began pushing at the big stone until they twirled it round. At first, when little Kâgssagssuk tried, he simply fell backwards.

'Now once more. Make haste, make haste, once more. And there again, there is a bigger one.'

And at last little Kâgssagssuk ceased to fall over backwards, and was able instead to move the stones and twirl them round. And each time he tried with a larger stone than before, and when he had succeeded with that, a larger one still. And so he kept on. And at last he could make even the biggest stones twirl round in the air, and the stone said *leu-leu-leu-leu* in the air.

Then said the giant at last, seeing that they were equal in strength:

'Now you have become a strong man. But since it was by my fault that you lost that piece of meat, I will by magic means cause bears to come down to your village. Three bears there will be, and they will come right down to the village.'

Then little Kâgssagssuk went home, and having returned home, went up to warm himself as usual at the smoke hole. Then came the master of that house, as usual, and hauled him

down by the nostrils. And afterwards, when he went to lie
down among the dogs, his wicked grandmother beat him and
them together, as was her custom. Altogether as if there
were no strong man in the village at all.

But in the night, when all were asleep, he went down to
one of the umiaks, which was frozen fast, and hauled it free.

Next morning when the men awoke, there was a great
to-do.

'*Hau!* That umiak has been hauled out of the ice!'

'*Hau!* There must be a strong man among us!'

'Who can it be that is so strong?'

'Here is the mighty one, without a doubt,' said
Umerdlugtoq, pointing to little Kâgssagssuk. But this he
said only in mockery.

And a little time after this, the people about the village

began to call out that three bears were in sight – exactly as the giant had said. Kâgssagssuk was inside, drying his boots. And while all the others were shouting eagerly about the place, he said humbly: 'If only I could borrow a pair of indoor boots from someone.'

And at last, as he could get no others, he was obliged to take his grandmother's boots and put them on.

Then he went out, and ran off over the hard-trodden snow outside the houses, treading with such force that it seemed as if

the footmarks were made in soft snow. And thus he went off
to meet the bears.

'*Hau!* Look at Kâgssagssuk. Did you ever see . . .'

'What is come to Kâgssagssuk; what can it be?'

Umerdlugtoq was greatly excited, and so astonished that
his eyes would not leave the boy. But little Kâgssagssuk
grasped the biggest of the bears – a mother with two half-
grown cubs – grasped that bear with his naked fists, and
wrung its neck, so that it fell down dead. Then he took those
cubs by the back of the neck and hammered their skulls
together until they too were dead.

Then little Kâgssagssuk went back homeward with the
biggest bear over his shoulders, and one cub under each arm,
as if they had been no more than hares. Thus he brought
them up to the house, and skinned them; then he set about
building a fireplace large enough to put a man in. For he was
now going to cook bears' meat for his grandmother, on a big
flat stone.

Umerdlugtoq, that great man, now made haste to get
away, taking his wives with him.

And Kâgssagssuk took that old grandmother who was
wont to beat him, and cast her on the fire, and she burned all
up till only her stomach was left. His other grandmother was
about to run away, but he held her back, and said:

'I shall now be kind to you, for you always used to dry my
boots.'

Now when Kâgssagssuk had made a meal of the bears'
meat, he set off in chase of those who had fled away. Umerdlugtoq had halted upon the top of a high hill, just on the
edge of a precipice, and had pitched their tent close to the
edge.

Up came Kâgssagssuk behind him, caught him by the
nostrils and held him out over the edge, and shook him so
violently that his nostrils burst. And there stood Umerdlugtoq holding his nose. But Kâgssagssuk said to him:

'Do not fear; I am not going to kill you. For you never

used to kill me.' And then little Kâgssagssuk went into the tent, and called out to him:

'Hi, come and look! I am in here with your wives!'

For in the old days, Umerdlugtoq had dared him even to look at them.

And having thus taken due vengeance, Kâgssagssuk went back to his village, and took vengeance there on all those who had ever ill-treated him. And some time after, he went away to the southward and lived with the people there.

Adam Bell, Clym of the Clough, and William of Cloudesley

Edited by WILLIAM MAYNE

I wondered whether to have Robin Hood among these stories; and in the end I decided not to, partly because he is so well known, and partly because he is too well known, and partly because I was never myself a great deal in sympathy with him. I am sure he is a hero in the sense I have tried to use in this collection; but I have never felt that he was a hero with much wonder round him. All the stories have the one motive, which seems like an early form of politics to me, taxing one lot of people in a rather unfair way, and giving to others. No doubt there was right on Robin's side; but equally there was right on the Sheriff of Nottingham's. So it was sad when Robin died, but it will have been peaceful too. I chose instead to use an old ballad about a similar character. First I thought I might turn it into a story; but as I went on trying to do so the verse itself cried out to stay as it was. So I have left it as it was, except for missing a section here and there (and I have mostly said so) and putting in modern spelling. If there is a word that is not known now, I have made a note; and a note or two about who is talking from time to time. I like the first part of the story best, the capture and the fight (which I admit is probably wrong-doing); and I like less the end of the story when William goes to the King. I have done most of the skipping in that part of the story; but I had to have it to round off the tale.

Merry it was in the green forest
Among the leavès green,
Wherein men hunt east and west
With bows and arrows keen;

To raise the deer out of their den;
Such sights have oft been seen;

As by three yeomen of the north country,
By them it is I mean.

The one of them hight¹ Adam Bell,   ¹ *hight*|named
The other Clym of the Clough,
The third was William of Cloudesley,
An archer good enough.

They were outlawed for venison,
These yeomen every one;
They swore them brethren upon a day,
To Inglewood for to gone.

Now lith² and listen, gentlemen,   ² *lith*|hearken
That of stories loveth to hear:
Two of them were single men,
The third had a wedded fere.³   ³ *fere*|wife

William was the wedded man,
Much more then was his care:
He said to his brethren upon a day,
To Carlisle he would fare;

For to speak with fair Alice his wife,
And with his children three.
'By my troth,' said Adam Bell,
'Not by the counsel of me:

'For if you go to Carlisle, brother,
And from this wild wood wend,
If that the Justice may you take,
Your life were at an end.'

William now speaks:

'If that I come not tomorrow, brother,
By Prime⁴ to you again,   ⁴ *Prime*|six in the morning
Trust you then that I am taken,
Or else that I am slain.'

He took his leave of his brethren two,
And to Carlisle he is gone:
There he knocked at his own window
Shortly and anon.

'Where be you, fair Alice,' he said,
'My wife and children three?
Lightly let in thine own husband,
William of Cloudesley.'

'Alas,' then said fair Alice,
And sighèd wondrous sore,
'This place hath been beset for you
For half a year and more.'

'Now I am here,' said Cloudesley,
'I would that in I were.
Now fetch us meat and drink enough,
And let us make good cheer.'

She fetchèd him meat and drink plenty,
Like a true wedded wife;
And pleasèd him with what she had,
Whom she lovèd as her life.

There lay an old wife in that place,
A little beside the fire,
Which William had found⁵ of charity   5 *found*|lodged and kept
More than seven year.

Up she rose and forth she goes
Evil might she speed therefore!
For she had set no foot on ground
In seven year before.

She went unto the Justice Hall,
As fast as she could hie:
'This night,' she said, 'is come to town
William of Cloudesley.'

Thereof the Justice was full fain,[6]   [6] *fain*|glad
And so was the Sheriff also:
'Thou shalt not travaile[7] hither, dame, for nought,   [7] *travaile*|work
Thy meed[8] thou shalt have or[9] thou go.'   [8] *meed*|reward
                                                          [9] *or*|before

They raised the town of merry Carlisle
In all the haste they can;
And came thronging to William's house,
As fast as they might gan.[10]   [10] *gan*|go

There they beset that good yeoman
Roundabout on every side:
William heard great noise of folks,
That hitherward fast hied.

Alice opened a back window.
And lookèd all about;
She was ware of the Justice and Sheriff both,
With a full great rout.[11]   [11] *rout*|crowd

'Alas, treason,' cried Alice,
'Ever woe may thou be.
Go into my chamber, my husband,' she said,
'Sweet William of Cloudesley.'

He took his sword and his buckler,
His bow and his children three,
And went into his strongest chamber,
Where he thought surest to be.

Fair Alice, like a lover true,
Took a pole-axe in her hand:
Said, 'He shall die that cometh in
This door, while I may stand.'

Cloudesley bent a well good bow,
That was of a trusty tree,
He smote the Justice on the breast,
That his arrow brast[12] in three.   [12] *brast*|broke

'God's curse on his heart,' said William,
'This day thy coat did on.
If it had been no better than mine,
It had gone near thy bone.'

'Yield thee, Cloudesley,' said the Justice,
'And thy bow and thy arrows thee fro.'[13]   [13] fro|from
'God's curse on his heart,' said fair Alice,
'That my husband counselleth so.'

'Set fire on the house,' said the Sheriff,
'Since it will no better be,
And burn we therein William,' he said,
'His wife and children three.'

They fired the house in many a place,
The fire flew up on high:
'Alas,' then cried fair Alice,
'I see we here shall die.'

William opened a back window,
That was in his chamber high,
And there with sheets he did let down
His wife and children three.

'Have you here my treasure,' said William,
'My wife and children three:
For Christès love do them no harm,
But wreak you all on me.'

William shot so wondrous well,
Till his arrows were all ago,[14]   [14] ago|agone
And the fire so fast upon him fell,
That his bowstring burnt in two.

The sparks burnt and fell upon
Good William of Cloudesley:
Then was he a woeful man, and said,
'This is a coward's death to me.

'Leifer[15] had I,' said William,   [15] leifer|rather
'With my sword in the rout to run,
Than here among mine enemies wood[16]   [16] wood|wild
Thus cruelly to burn.'

He took his sword and his buckler,
And among them all he ran,
Where the people were most in press,
He smote down many a man.

There might no man abide his strokes,
So fiercely on them he ran:
Then they threw windows and doors on him,
And so took that good yeoman.

There they him bounde both hand and foot,
And in a deep dungeon him cast:
'Now Cloudesley,' said the Justice,
'Thou shalt be hangèd in haste.'

'A pair of new gallows,' said the Sheriff,
'Now shall I for thee make;
And the gates of Carlisle shall be shut:
No man shall come in thereat.

'They shall not help Clym of the Clough,
Nor yet shall Adam Bell,
Though they came with a thousand more,
Nor all the devils in Hell.'

Early in the morning the Justice arose,
To the gates first can he gone.
And commanded to be shut full close
Lightly every one.

Then went he to the market place,
As fast as he could hie;
There a pair of new gallows he set up
Beside the pillory.

A little boy among them asked,
What meanèd that gallow tree?
They said, to hang a good yeoman,
Called William of Cloudesley.

The little boy was the town swine-herd,
And kept fair Alice's swine;
Oft had he seen William in the wood,
And given him there to dine.[17]   [17] *dine*|brought food to him

He went out at a crevice of the wall,
And lightly to the wood did gone;
There met he with these wight yeomen
Shortly and anon.

'Alas,' then said the little boy,
'Ye tarry here all too long;
Cloudesley is taken, and damned to death,
And ready for to hang.'

'Alas,' then said good Adam Bell,
'That ever we saw this day.
He had better had tarrièd with us,
So oft as we did him pray.

'He might have dwelt in green forest,
Under the shadows green,
And have kept both him and us at rest,
Out of all trouble and teen.'[18]   [18] *teen*|bother and sorrow

Adam bent a right good bow,
A great hart soon had he slain:
'Take that, child, to thy dinner,
And bring me my arrow again.'

'Now go we hence,' said these wight yeoman,
'Tarry we no longer here;
We shall him borrow by God his grace,
Though it we buy full dear.'

And when they came to merry Carlisle,
In a fair good morning tide,
They found the gates shut them until[19]   [19] *until|unto*
About on every side.

'Alas,' then said good Adam Bell,
'That ever we were made men.
These gates be shut so wonderly well,
We may not come therein.'

Now Adam Bell and Clym of the Clough trick the porter
by pretending to be messengers from the King with a letter.
The porter opens the gates, and has his neck wrung for his
pains, and his keys taken from him.

'Now I am porter,' said Adam Bell,
'See, brother, the keys are here,
The worst porter to merry Carlisle
That they had this hundred year.

'And now will we our bowès bend,
Into the town will we go,
For to deliver our dear brother,
That lieth in care and woe.'

And Cloudesley lay ready in a cart,
Fast bound both foot and hand;
And a strong rope about his neck,
All ready for to be hanged.

The Justice called to him a lad,
Cloudesley's clothes should he have,
To take the measure of that yeoman,
Thereafter to make his grave.

'I have seen as great marvel,' said Cloudesley,
'As between this and prime,
He that maketh a grave for me,
Himself may lie therein.'

'Thou speakest proudly,' said the Justice,
'I will hang thee with my hand.'
Full well heard this the brethren two,
There still as they did stand.

Then Cloudesley cast his eyes aside
And saw his brethren stand
At a corner of the market place,
With their good bows bent in their hand.

They loosed their arrows both at once,
Of no man had they dread;
The one hit the Justice, the other the Sheriff,
That both their sides gan[20] bleed.

[20] gan|began

All men voided,[21] them that stood nigh,
When the Justice fell to the ground,
And the Sheriff fell nigh him by;
Either had his death wound.

[21] voided|ran away

All the citizens fast gan fly.
They durst no longer bide:
There lightly they loosèd Cloudesley,
Where he with ropes lay tied.

William said to his brethren two,
'This day let us live and die,
If e'er you have need, as I have now,
The same you shall find by me.'

They shot so well in that tide
(Their strings were of silk, full sure)
That they kept the streets on every side;
That battle did long endure.

They fought together as brethren true,
Like hardy men and bold,
Many a man to the ground they threw,
And many a heart made cold.

But when their arrows were all gone,
Men pressèd to them full fast,
They drew their swordès then anon,
And their bows from them cast.

They went lightly on their way,
With swords and bucklers round,
But that it was mid of the day,
They had made many a wound.

There was many an out-horn in Carlisle blown,
And the bells backward did ring;
Many a woman said Alas,
And many their hands did wring.

The Mayor of Carlisle forth come was,
With him a full great rout:
These three yeomen dread him full sore,
For their livès stood in doubt.

The Mayor came armèd a full great pace,²²   ²² *pace* | quickly
With a pole-axe in his hand;
Many a strong man with him was,
There in that stour²³ to stand.   ²³ *stour* | fighting crowd

The Mayor smote at Cloudesley with his bill,
His buckler he brast in two,
Full many a yeoman with great ill,
'Alas, Treason!' they cried for woe.
'Keep the gates fast we will,
That these traitors thereout not go.'

But all for nought was that they wrought,
For so fast they down were laid,
Till they all three, that so manfully fought
Were gotten without, at a braide.²⁴   ²⁴ *braide* | sudden leap

'Have here your keys,' said Adam Bell,
'Mine office I here forsake;
And if you do by my counsell
A new porter do ye make.'

He threw their keys there at their heads,
And bade them well to thrive,
And all that letteth²⁵ any good yeoman   ²⁵ *letteth* | hindereth
To come and comfort his wife.

Thus be these good yeomen gone to the wood
As lightly as leaf on lind,²⁶   ²⁶ *lind* | linden tree

They laugh and be merry in their mood,
Their enemies were far behind.

They come upon their store of arrows, and they wish they
were back in Carlisle still fighting. Fair Alice and the children
are found in the wood, too. Afterwards William and his
brethren go to the King's court, and confess to killing deer.
The King orders them to be hanged, but the Queen inter-
cedes. Messengers come from Carlisle, to say that the Justice
and the Sheriff are dead, and who killed them. The King
wishes to see how these men shoot, who killed three hundred
of his subjects. They go to shoot, and William proves his
skill by putting an apple on the head of his eldest son, turning
the child's face away so that he would not see the arrow
coming and move. He shoots the apple in two, and the King
says, 'God forbid that thou shouldst shoot at me,' and gives
him eighteenpence a day to be chief range-rider of the north
country, and the Queen gives him thirteenpence too, and he
and his brethren are made into gentlemen, and the eldest son
given work and the promise of advancement. They 'died
good men all three'.

Thus ended the lives of these good yeomen;
God send them eternal bliss;
And all, that with a hand-bow shooteth:
That of heaven they may never miss.

Sea Heroes

This is a bundle of sea-going heroes. Sir Francis Drake, first, who is the greatest of them all, not only for what he did but for what people (especially the Spaniards) thought he did. He was a great enemy to them in Elizabethan times, and they thought he could order the wind about, and that he had a glass in his cabin that showed him the positions of the Spanish ships. He was supposed to be a magician, both by the enemy and by his own countrymen, and legends have risen after him: there is a drum that was his, and is said to sound by itself when the country is in danger. Stories add themselves to people like Drake, because he had the heroic quality.

Sir Richard Grenville was a contemporary of Drake, and fought the same enemy. He fought the Armada with him, and like him sailed to the New World and attacked Spanish treasure ships. At his last battle Grenville was lying in wait in the Azores when he heard that a big battle fleet was coming to meet the treasure ships. There was some delay in getting away from the harbour, and Grenville tried to slip through the fifty-three warships that had just come from Spain. But he was caught, and in his little ship, with one hundred and ninety men, he fought for fifteen hours against fifteen Spanish ships and five thousand men. He lost the battle in the end, and himself died a few days later on the Spanish flagship.

John Paul Jones was a Scotsman who perfectly honourably found himself on the American side in the War of Independence in the 1760s. The war was lost by England. During it John Paul Jones sailed back to England and pirated round the coasts, and was in a battle off Scarborough, which is particularly remembered. The verse in this section is about that, though it calls the North Sea the English Channel (the poet lived far away in America). So that I don't leave an impression that American ships had everything their own way in the war, there follows another piece about a sea fight near Boston between the English ship 'Shannon' (with thirty-eight guns) and the American 'Chesapeake' (with forty-nine guns).

The Old Navy is about wars against France. It seems to be a sort of pep talk given by the captain before battle began, to urge them to be heroes in the fight, or take the consequences (a flogging).

OF THE GREAT AND FAMOUS

Ever to be honoured Knight, Sir Francis Drake, and of my
little-little selfe

ROBERT HAYMAN

The Dragon that o'er Seas did raise his Crest
And brought back heapes of gold unto his nest,
Unto his Foes more terrible than Thunder,
Glory of his age, After-ages' wonder,
Excelling all those that excelled before;
It's feared we shall have none such any more;
Effecting all he sole did undertake,
Valiant, just, wise, milde, honest, Godly Drake.
This man when I was little I did meete
As he was walking up Totnes' long street.
He asked me whose I was? I answered him.
He asked me if his good friend were within?
A faire red Orange in his hand he had,
He gave it me whereof I was right glad,
Takes and kist me, and prayes God blesse my boy:
Which I record with comfort to this day.
Could he on me have breathèd with his breath,
His gifts, Elias-like, after his death,
Then had I beene enabled for to doe
Many brave things I have a heart unto.
I have as great desire as e'er had hee
To joy, annoy, friends, foes; but 'twill not be.

DRAKE'S CANNON BALL

RUTH L. TONGUE

There were one o' the Sydenham maids, and 'er got 'erself
betrothed to Sir Francis Drake. But afore they could be

married 'e 'ad to go away on a voyage, and 'ow long it'd be afore 'e could come back, no one knew, and 'e didn't trust 'er father. So they took their troth-plight, the two of 'en, afore Drake sailed away. Well, 'e sailed away, for three long years, and Sir George Sydenham, 'e found another suitor for 'is daughter, a much richer one. Well, no matter what the maid do say, marriage were announced and she were half afraid o' Sir Francis Drake, but she were more afraid of 'er father. So she give in.

Well now, Sir Francis Drake, 'e did do some very strange things – 'e did sit on Plymouth 'oe, a-whittling of a stick, and all the chips that fell into the sea, they did turn into ships, to go fight the Spanish Armada. Now, although 'e'd been gone three years, 'e knew what was 'appening, so at the very door o' the church, 'e dropped a red-'ot cannon ball in front o' the bridal party. Oh! give 'en a fright, did – and when 'e come 'ome at last, 'twas to find 'is bride and 'er dear father a-waiting for 'en with smiles. As for t'other bridegroom, 'e'd a-taken 'isself across the length and breadth of England. But I expect Sir Francis Drake knew where 'e was tew!

THE REVENGE

LORD TENNYSON

At Flores in the Azores Sir Richard Grenville lay,
And a pinnace, like a flutter'd bird, came flying from far away:
'Spanish ships of war at sea! we have sighted fifty-three!'
Then sware Lord Thomas Howard: ''Fore God I am no
     coward;
But I cannot meet them here, for my ships are out of gear,
And the half my men are sick. I must fly, but follow quick.
We are six ships of the line; can we fight with fifty-three?'

Then spake Sir Richard Grenville: 'I know you are no coward;
You fly them for a moment to fight with them again.
But I've ninety men and more that are lying sick ashore.
I should count myself the coward if I left them, my Lord
     Howard,
To these Inquisition dogs and the devildoms of Spain.'

So Lord Howard past away with five ships of war that day,
Till he melted like a cloud in the silent summer heaven;
But Sir Richard bore in hand all his sick men from the land
Very carefully and slow,
Men of Bideford in Devon,
And we laid them on the ballast down below;
For we brought them all aboard,
And they blest him in their pain, that they were not left to
     Spain,
To the thumbscrew and the stake, for the glory of the Lord.

He had only a hundred seamen to work the ship and to fight,
And he sailed away from Flores till the Spaniard came in sight,
With his huge sea-castles heaving upon the weather-bow.
'Shall we fight or shall we fly?
Good Sir Richard, tell us now,
For to fight is but to die!
There'll be little of us left by the time this sun be set.'
And Sir Richard said again: 'We be all good Englishmen.
Let us bang these dogs of Seville, the children of the devil,
For I never turn'd my back upon Don or devil yet.'

Sir Richard spoke and he laugh'd, and we roar'd a hurrah,
     and so
The little Revenge ran on sheer into the heart of the foe,
With her hundred fighters on deck, and her ninety sick below;
For half of their fleet to the right and half to the left were seen,
And the little Revenge ran on thro' the long sea-lane between.
Thousands of their soldiers look'd down from their decks and
     laugh'd,
Thousands of their seamen made mock at the mad little craft

Running on and on, till delay'd
By their mountain-like San Philip that, of fifteen hundred tons,
And up-shadowing high above us with her yawning tiers of guns,
Took the breath from our sails, and we stay'd.

And while now the great San Philip *hung above us like a*
    cloud
Whence the thunderbolt will fall
Long and loud,
Four galleons drew away
From the Spanish fleet that day,
And two upon the larboard and two upon the starboard lay,
And the battle-thunder broke from them all.

But anon the great San Philip, *she bethought herself and went*
Having that within her womb that had left her ill content;
And the rest they came aboard us, and they fought us hand to
    hand,
For a dozen times they came with their pikes and musqueteers,
And a dozen times we shook 'em off as a dog that shakes his
    ears
When he leaps from the water to the land.

And the sun went down, and the stars came out far over the
    summer sea,
But never a moment ceased the fight of the one and the fifty-
    three.
Ship after ship, the whole night long, their high-built galleons
    came,
Ship after ship, the whole night long, with her battle-thunder
    and flame;

Ship after ship, the whole night long, drew back with her dead
    and her shame.
For some were sunk and many were shatter'd, and so could
    fight us no more –
God of battles, was ever a battle like this in the world before?

For he said 'Fight on! fight on!'
Tho' his vessel was all but a wreck;
And it chanced that, when half of the short summer night was
    gone,
With a grisly wound to be drest he had left the deck,

But a bullet struck him that was dressing it suddenly dead,
And himself he was wounded again in the side and the head,
And he said 'Fight on! fight on!'

And the night went down, and the sun smiled out far over the
        summer sea,
And the Spanish fleet with broken sides lay round us all in a
        ring;
But they dared not touch us again, for they fear'd that we still
        could sting,
So they watch'd what the end would be.
And we had not fought them in vain,
But in perilous plight were we,
Seeing forty of our poor hundred were slain,
And half of the rest of us maim'd for life
In the crash of the cannonades and the desperate strife;
And the sick men down in the hold were most of them stark
        and cold,
And the pikes were all broken or bent, and the powder was all
        of it spent;
And the masts and the rigging were lying over the side;
But Sir Richard cried in his English pride,
'We have fought such a fight for a day and a night
As may never be fought again!'

'We have won great glory, my men!
And a day less or more
At sea or ashore,
We die – does it matter when?
Sink me the ship, Master Gunner – sink her, split her in twain!
Fall into the hands of God, not into the hands of Spain!'
And the gunner said 'Ay, ay,' but the seamen made reply:
'We have children, we have wives,
And the Lord hath spared our lives.
We will make the Spaniard promise, if we yield, to let us go;
We shall live to fight again and to strike another blow.'
And the lion there lay dying, and they yielded to the foe.

And the stately Spanish men to their flagship bore him then,
Where they laid him by the mast, old Sir Richard caught at
　　　last,
And they praised him to his face with their courtly foreign
　　　grace;
But he rose upon their decks, and he cried:
'I have fought for Queen and Faith like a valiant man and
　　　true;

I have only done my duty as a man is bound to do:
With a joyful spirit I Sir Richard Grenville die!'
And he fell upon their decks, and he died.

And they stared at the dead that had been so valiant and true,
And had holden the power and glory of Spain so cheap
That he dared her with one little ship and his English few;
Was he devil or man? He was devil for aught they knew,
But they sank his body with honour down into the deep,
And they mann'd the Revenge with a swarthier alien crew,
And away she sail'd with her loss and long'd for her own;
When a wind from the lands they had ruin'd awoke from sleep,

And the water began to heave and the weather to moan,
And or ever that evening ended a great gale blew,
And a wave like the wave that is raised by an earthquake grew,
Till it smote on their hulls and their sails and their masts and
their flags,
And the whole sea plunged and fell on the shot-shatter'd navy
of Spain,
And the little Revenge herself went down by the island crags
To be lost evermore in the main.

PAUL JONES

ANONYMOUS

An American Frigate, call'd the Richard by name
Mounted guns forty-four, from New York she came,
To cruise in the channel of old England's fame,
With a noble commander, Paul Jones was his name.

We had not cruised long, before two sails we espied
A large forty-four, and a twenty likewise,
With fifty bright shipping, well loaded with stores,
And the convoy stood in for Old Yorkshire's shore.

'Bout the hour of twelve, we came alongside,
With a long speaking trumpet, whence came you he cried,
Come answer me quickly, or I'll hail you no more,
Or else a broadside into you I will pour.

We fought them four glasses, four glasses so hot,
Till forty bold seamen lay dead on the spot
And fifty-five more lay bleeding in gore,
While the thund'ring large cannons of Paul Jones did roar.

Our carpenter being frightened, to Paul Jones did say,
Our ship leaks water, since fighting today,
Paul Jones made answer, in the height of his pride,
If we can do no better we'll sink alongside.

Paul Jones he then smiled and to his men did say,
Let every man stand the best of his play,
For broadside for broadside they fought on the main,
Like true British heroes we return'd it again.

The Seraphis wore round our ship for to rake,
Which made the proud hearts of the English to ache,
The shot flew so hot we could not stand it long,
Till the bold British colours from the English came down.

Oh now my brave boys we have taken a rich prize,
A large forty-four and a twenty likewise,
Help the poor mothers that have reason to weep
At the loss of their sons in the unfathomed deep.

THE 'SHANNON' AND THE 'CHESAPEAKE'

ANONYMOUS

On board the Shannon frigate,
In the merry month of May,

To watch those bold *Americans*,
   Off *Boston* lights we lay.
The Chesapeake *was in harbour*,
   A frigate stout and fine –
Four hundred and forty men had she,
   Her guns were forty-nine.

'Twas Captain Broke commanded us –
   A challenge he did write
To the captain of the Chesapeake,
   To bring her out to fight:
Our captain says – 'Brave Lawrence,
   'Tis not from enmity;
But 'tis to prove to all the world
   That we do rule the sea.

'Don't think, my noble captain,
   Because you've had success,
That British tars are humbled –
   Not even in distress.
No! we will fight like heroes,
   Our glory to maintain,
In defiance of your greater size
   And the number of your men.'

That challenge was accepted;
   The Americans came down –
A finer frigate ne'er belonged
   Unto the British crown.
They brought her into action,
   On our true English plan;
Nor fired a shot till within hail –
   And then the hell began.

Broadside for broadside quick
   Set up a murderous roar;
Like thunder it resounded
   From echoing shore to shore.

This dreadful duel lasted
  Near a quarter-of-an-hour;
Then the Chesapeake drove right aboard,
  And put her in our power.

Our captain went to their ship's side
  To see how she did lie,
When he beheld the enemy's men,
  Who from their guns did fly.
'All hands for boarding!' now he cried.
  'The victory is sure!
Come, bear a hand, my gallant boys –
  Our prize we'll now secure!'

Like lions then we rushed aboard,
  And fought them hand to hand;
And tho' they did outnumber us,
  They could not us withstand.
They fought in desperation,
  Disorder and dismay,
And in about three minutes' time
  Were forced to give us way.

Their captain and lieutenant,
  With seventy of the crew,
Were killed in this sharp action,
  And a hundred wounded too;
The ship we took to Halifax,
  And the captain buried there,
And the living of his crew
  And his chief mourners were.

Have courage, all brave British tars,
  And never be dismayed;
But put the can of grog about,
  And drink success to trade;
Likewise to gallant Captain Broke
  And all his valiant crew,

Who beat the bold Americans
And brought their courage to.

THE OLD NAVY

CAPTAIN CHARLES MARRYAT

The captain stood on the carronade: 'First lieutenant,' says he,
'Send all my merry men aft here, for they must list to me;
I haven't the gift of the gab, my sons – because I'm bred to the
    sea;
That ship there is a Frenchman, who means to fight with we.
    And odds bobs, hammer and tongs, long as I've been to sea,
    I've fought 'gainst every odds – but I've gained the victory!

'That ship there is a Frenchman, and if we don't take she,
'Tis a thousand bullets to one, that she will capture we;
I haven't the gift of the gab, my boys; so each man to his gun;
If she's not mine in half an hour, I'll flog each mother's son.
    For odds bobs, hammer and tongs, long as I've been to sea,
    I've fought 'gainst every odds – and I've gained the victory!'

We fought for twenty minutes, when the Frenchman had enough;
'I little thought,' said he, 'that your men were of such stuff;'
Our captain took the Frenchman's sword, a low bow made to he;
'I haven't the gift of the gab, monsieur, but polite I wish to be.
    And odds bobs, hammer and tongs, long as I've been to sea,
    I've fought 'gainst every odds – and I've gained the victory!'

Our captain sent for all of us: 'My merry men,' said he,
'I haven't the gift of the gab, my lads, but yet I thankful be:
You've done your duty handsomely, each man stood to his gun;
If you hadn't, you villains, as sure as day, I'd have flogged each
    mother's son,
    For odds bobs, hammer and tongs, as long as I'm at sea,
    I'll fight 'gainst every odds – and I'll gain the victory!'

Sir Perceval

Retold by WILLIAM MAYNE

King Arthur is the top hero of the world, and I have said so many times. But I thought you might by now know that; so when it came to putting in a piece about him, I thought it best to step aside a little, and have King Arthur as a minor character, almost as a background person, and let Perceval be the middle of it all. There are many tales about Perceval, or Parzifal, spread about the edges of Europe, and they all start with much the same thing, a retired childhood, and great nobility later, in spite of his mother's entreaties (she is usually a widowed countess). I have followed the lines of the story as it is set out in the works of Thomas Bulfinch, a man very useful to anyone looking at mythology at all. He was an American, born late in the eighteenth century, and he set down a great mass of work in a way that is still readable. But I thought it was not quite up-to-date, somehow, and I took ideas and plots from him, both for this, and for other stories. But elsewhere in this book is 'The Battle of Roncesvalles', which is by Thomas Bulfinch himself.

Now there was a big lad that lived once-over at the top of the dale, maybe at Lunds or Fleet Moss, or again it may be Langstrothdale. However, it was a far out spot, and no wonder he grew up a yonderly lad.

First then, there was no man to the house. There was his mother, and a woman or two; and they were the only keeping he had with the world. So lambing and haytime alike he was brought up like a farm lad.

There was no man to the house, because his father had been killed in fight before he was born and breathed day. And his mother was a Scottish queen, who came away then out of her own country and lived quietly far from the world.

The fight that killed her man was in her mind week by week and month by month and year by year. So there was to be no sort of fighting for the lad. Nothing was shown to him that could mean harm to any man, and all he had was a little Scottish spear, and with that he would chase the rabbits.

His father's blood was in him, whatever his mother did; and after the boy chased the rabbits, the youth went after the deer, and the young man went after the wild pig, all with the little Scottish spear, because he was a big lad, and a strong lad. And he had the eye of a buzzard, so that his little spear would hit a flying bird and bring it down.

He was ranging the tops one day when he came on five horse-riders. Now that was a thing he never had seen; and the horses at the farm were fell ponies that led wood and drew the haysledge, and never had man on their backs.

And more than the riding was the manner of the riders, and their covering. It was black steel, with gold edges and red feathers, and helmets like rocks on a gatepost, and spears like the balks of a haymew, and saddles like a great chair, and at their sides singing swords.

The big lad saw big fellows, that was all, and shouted to them. 'Hey,' he said, 'get away off our pasture.' And they halted in their ride, and looked at him, and their steel flashed. The big lad ran away, because he never saw steel before that day. He ran home, and found his mother.

'Mother,' he said, 'what's these fellows I've seen?' And he told her of the blackness and the red and the gold and the steel.

'Whisht,' said his mother, before he had done. 'It was angels.'

'Then I will be an angel with them,' said the lad.

'Away,' said his mother, 'come away here and get your dinner. I have not brought you here to be an angel.'

So the big lad took his dinner. But he was his father's son, though they never saw each other; and he knew that he was to be an angel. So when he had eaten and drunk, he took his little spear again and went on the tops, and found the five horse-riders. They were off their horses, and taking their own dinners, sat against a rock. But they were ready for him, and before he was past them there were five points towards his heart, and the sun flashing on every one as he looked round. So he dropped his little Scottish spear, that was made of wood, and stood still.

'I have come to be an angel,' he said. 'If thou will tell me what to study.'

Said one horse-rider to another: 'This is the big lad that shouted of us to be out of his pasture not long since. If he had known what we were he would not have done so.'

'No, indeed,' said the big lad. 'I thought you were men, and now I know you are angels, and my mother has taught me that though angels are lower than men because they are not made in the likeness of God, yet they are more honourable because they have seen God. So I beg you tell not God that I shouted at you.'

'For that,' said one of the riders, 'God sees all. And for that again, we are not angels, but still we are honourable. Now lad, sit down on this rock, and we will take our swords from your

heart and eat our dinners. And tell us first what is your name? And who is your father? And why does a big lad like you have only a little Scottish spear to his hand, morning and afternoon?'

The big lad said his name was Perceval; and he would have told them who his father was, but he did not know; and he would have told them who his mother was, but she had not said she was a queen; and he would have told them why he had only a little spear, but he did not know why he should have any other, when there were only small creatures to be caught.

So they listened to him, and then they asked him why he did not follow the honourable course of knighthood. 'We are knights,' they said, 'and follow our course wherever it is set, and come again to the court of the king, Arthur, when the time is right, and sit again at the round table and have good company and fellowship. But you will never be a knight with a little Scottish spear.'

'Then tell me,' said Perceval, 'what I must have; for, whether you are angels or knights, now that I have seen you, I want to be in no other way in the world but the way you are in, and to be such as you.'

And they told him then that the way was hard, and the reward of being a knight not easily come by, and that first he must present himself ready at court, to see how the king thought of him.

'I'll be on,' said Perceval, 'maybe not so fast, but I'll be on.' And he took up his little spear, and laid it against the great spears of the knights. 'Shall I come with my little Scottish spear, or shall I make one like yours?' he said.

Then he looked upon their horses, and touched this part and that of the horses' gear, saying, 'What's thou call this, and this, and this that you have your iron feet in? And what is the yellow iron that shines on you and is brighter than the black iron?'

So they told him the names of the horses' gear, part for

part, bridle and girth and stirrup; and the yellow iron, they said was common gold. And then the knights went their own road, and Perceval went his, and came down home again, bringing the little spear with him.

He laid it aside, and went to the two ponies that were outside the house, and brought heavy stuff, and had never had man or woman on their backs; and he chose the taller one. 'Thou must ride under me,' he said, 'and take me to the king, and there thou will become an honourable horse, not a kitchen pony.'

And he brought a pack and made it into the form of a saddle, and tied it on the pony's back; and he took grass and he took twigs from the trees against the house, and worked them into a likeness of the fittings of the knights' horses, and hung them round the pony. And he took wood and made himself a coat like the iron coats of the knights, and hung it on himself; so that to see him you would say he was a great child; but he had nothing else he could use. And for sword and weapon he had only his little spear that would strike a flying bird.

When he had done these things, and was ready, he led the pony to the front side of the house, and found his mother.

'I's off,' he said. 'Them fellows wasn't angels, sithee, but knights, and they join of a big company that lives with the king; and I've gitten myself dressed like them, and I's off.'

His mother saw that her years of peaceful living had gone for nothing; that Perceval would be off towards the wars and fighting, and she was force put to let him go. But, 'Nay lad,' she said. 'Thou stop home with thy mammy and keep thy croft.'

'Now, Mother,' said Perceval, 'I's off, choose how,' and off he went; but not before he had a clean shirt and his mother had told him some things:

'Your father,' she said, 'was a great knight, and worthy of any man in Arthur's court. Yet he died himself before thou was born. But his blood was woken in you. Go to the king, and ask him to make you a knight, and follow his laws. But for me, remember that at each church and chapel say a prayer. And since you are travelling to be a knight, then you may take food and drink as you need them, but no more; and in return you have a duty on you to help all who need help and who cry for it; and you have a duty to win fame for yourself and the king; so, if you see a fair jewel, then win it, which will bring you a good name; and be ready to give it to any other person in turn, because that will bring you a better name. And it is your duty as a knight to marry a fine woman, so that you must pay court to one if you can, ready against the time when you are made knight.'

'I will do these things in their turn,' said Perceval. And then he rode over the hill, out of Langstrothdale, towards the city of the king. And by night-time he had seen no man and no house, nothing for his spear, and he laid himself to sleep in the ling like a badger.

In the morning he drank out of a beck, and that was his meat for the day. And he slept in a woodland. And on the third day he found the tent of a woman that kept pigs, that was a wandering woman of her wandering tribe, out on the fell to keep her herd. All her tribe lived in the mud with their pigs. But Perceval thought she was very bonny.

'I's glad to see thee,' he said, and sat in the mouth of the tent and smelt the fire; as well he might, with the ribs of pig roasting on it. And the woman said nothing to him, because there was not a word between them that they knew. And Perceval remembered that he could eat what he found so he ate the ribs of pig from the fire, and he drank the barley beer the pig tribe made, and he slept at the tent mouth. And the woman had pity on him, because he was young and his skin pink, like a new pig; so that when her tribe began to call and to come to her she woke Perceval and pushed him away, because the pig tribe would kill him for being on their land. So Perceval went unharmed, and before he went he took his own ring from his finger, and he took the ring from the woman's finger that was fine gold from a beck, and changed them one for the other, because that was a fair jewel, and he was giving away his own fair jewel. And he mounted his pony and rode on.

Then he came to the camp of the king, where it is at in the south-west part of the land, behind the walls the fairies made long before. The king was in his hall, and the curtain was on the doorstead. It was the hide of a horse hanging there, and the smoke at it and at the edges of the roof. Perceval said in his mind that the place was fired; yet there were the voices of men and women within, gathered together.

The big lad did as he would do in Langstrothdale, or where it was he came from; and that is, to walk in, friend and fearless, to shelter. And besides, he had no harm to him then. So on the wood-gathering pony he walked in, lifting the curtain aside with his arm, and going into the smoke.

Those that were in were well seasoned to it, and they could see. Perceval had been away from house reek many days, and his eyes began to teem, and he was blinded. And he thought he was deafed too, when quiet came on all that were in the hall.

In a little time he could see again; and he saw the gathering of resting men, and saw a quarrel. A big fellow that was more bold in the stomach than in the head with the drink he had, jerked the arm of the page boy that served the queen, so that the drink went on her face and her gown and not in the cup. The silence that came when Perceval rode in turned on the man who had insulted the queen. He stood up, with the drink talking, and said that if any there would be bold enough to avenge the insult, he would wait for them outside, and make a fight of it at the meadow. And off he went with the queen's cup.

'Time enough for him,' said a chiefly man that sat by the queen. 'Now what have we here? Who is this big lad?'

And another man came busily forward to see what the big lad was, and stood in the middle of the hall to see him better, and the firelight was no redder than the hair on his head.

'Now then, Lofty,' said Perceval, making the pleasant talk of his own country, because the man with red hair was short in his height, as short to Perceval as Perceval's pony was to a knight's horse. 'Now then, Lofty, which is t'gaffer? And what do they call thee?'

The man flickered with his tongue like a flame, but said no word. Then he said: 'You have fine manners, lad. My name is Kay. But what do you want with the king, Arthur?'

'My mammy sent me,' said Perceval. 'To be a knight.'

'You have a great horse for it,' said Kay. 'You would walk quicker without it, and run too, because your legs are longer than his; and you would be easier too, than set on a folded pack for a saddle, and woven about with twigs and grass like a bower. But, lad, that great spear you have more than makes up, and you would strike kingdoms dead with terror if you waved it in the air.' And Kay took the little Scottish spear and waved it in the air.

After Kay the rest of the people there began to laugh at him too, for his riding into the hall, for having a pony so small, for decking it with trappings of twigs and grass, for having wooden armour, and for talking with his own voice that was unknown to them.

One only did not laugh. There was a serving girl at the fire, who pitied Perceval, who would not laugh and jeer. In fact she had been a year in the king's household and had never smiled yet, so much that the appointed fool said she must be waiting for better knights than she had known before she would smile. Now she smiled at Perceval, and ran to him, and stood between him and Kay, to thwart Kay from his teasing mischief.

'Now missy,' said Kay. 'You have been told when to smile, so do not come grinning at the first lout that wanders in witless.'

And he lifted his hand and knocked her down, because he was a hasty, spiteful man; and of all the court only the serving girls and the pages were shorter than he when he stood on his own feet. On a horse, though, he was the equal of many, and the better of plenty.

'Go,' he said to Perceval, giving him back the little Scottish spear, 'go after that fellow that went out last, and bring that cup back here.'

So Perceval turned his pony close against the fire, and lifted the curtain and went out. The girl had run away, or he might have waited. But he went to look for the man that had the cup.

The man was in the meadow, clearing his head by the waterside, and the cup was hung in a willow tree. Perceval thought nothing to the man, but went for the cup. But as he reached for it the man cried out that he must stop, and fight first, if he wanted the cup.

'Nay, lad,' said Perceval. 'I was told it wanted fetching, so I've come for it.'

'And who told you that?' said the man. 'You are no knight.'

'Yon tall fellow,' said Perceval, 'him with the ginger knob. Haven't I to do what he says?'

'Get back in,' said the man, 'and tell Arthur to come and fight himself for it.'

'I'll take the cup first,' said Perceval. 'I can do nobbut yan thing at a time, sithee. I'll take t'cup, and t'gaffer can fight thee after.'

Then the man rode against him, and Perceval had to leave the cup for the time, and fight first. The man, with his long spear, thrust against Perceval's armour, and split the wood, so that he was bare-chested.

'This is a right game,' said Perceval. 'I'll knock thy end in, lad, and sharpish.' And he lifted his little Scottish spear and threw it. 'They play as rough as thee in t'dales,' he said. 'Thou watch.'

And the man watched too long, because the spear went in at his eye and out at the back of his head, and he was killed.

Then Perceval lifted the cup down. But he thought it

would not be seemly to go into the king's hall with his chest bare, so he set to to take the man's body armour off.

Owen came then from the hall, where he had talked with Kay, and told him it was wrong to send such a young lad to fight a fierce knight that had drink in him. 'It will disgrace us either way, for how can we let a knight be killed by such a fellow; and how could a knight honourably kill such a booby?' So Owen came himself to see.

He found Perceval in the meadow dragging the man about.

'What are you doing?' said Owen.

'It is this iron coat,' said Perceval. 'I can't get the beggar off whatever. By, it is fast on him.'

'Be easy then,' said Owen, 'and turn him on his side, and there, turn this, and this,' and between them they took out the smith's bolts that held the armour. 'Now,' said Owen, 'my dear fellow, this is better armour than your own, and a better horse, if you will allow me to say so. So put them on, and bring the cup you were sent for, and we'll go back to the hall and see what we can make of you.'

'Nay, I've been thinking,' said Perceval. 'I'll not come in that hall again yet, not until I've gitten myself ready to thump yon fellow Lofty, yon Ginger, thou'lt ken him, and given him t'thump back he gave that lass. He was never right to do that. But I've broken my lile spear, and I doubt I's not handy with these I've gained. Thou take t'cup, and say what I's off to do. And then, when I's master of the big spear I'll come on and see t'gaffer, and maybe get taken on.'

So Owen took the cup in, and told the men at the hall what had happened.

Perceval rode off again, and took him to a quiet place, and taught himself to ride the great horse, and to use the great spear, and to wield the great sword, so that he was ready to make the best of his adventures he could. There is a place for the telling of his adventures, but it is not here. There was the time in the magic boat, and there was the time when the river before him boiled, and there was fight after fight. At each fight the big lad would win, and the man he beat he sent back to the king's hall, to greet the king as lord, and to bring Perceval's own name forward. And there were sixteen knights that he sent back.

And the summer went by, and the autumn came, and then the winter, and with the winter the snow. Perceval came one night to the hut of a hermit, and lodged with him. And in the morning, when they came out of the hut, the snow was white over the hills, and the sky was blue with frost. And then a hawk stooped on a bird, and killed it on the snow, and blood lay there red. And when the hawk had gone a raven came, that the hermit would feed, and stood black against the snow. And Perceval compared all the colours to those of the maiden that had smiled only for him: the whiteness of the snow was like her skin, and the blackness of the raven was like her hair, and the blue of the sky was like her eyes, and the redness was like the redness of her cheeks.

And so he looked, and thought it was time he should return to the hall of the king; and he thought about the girl, and stood on the top of the hill like a tree.

The king, Arthur, was nearby, and saw Perceval on the hill, and wondered who the big lad was. One of the young men there said he would go and see. So he ran up the hill, and came close to Perceval, and said, 'Hey, who are you?'

But Perceval was thinking, and standing in the snow, and said nothing. So the young man touched him with his spear, though not the point. And Perceval lifted up one arm and gave the young man a blow and sent him into a snowdrift. And the young man crawled out and blew the snow from his mouth and came down again feeling his head.

Kay was there. 'I will go myself,' he said. 'It is no good sending anyone else, I can see.'

So he went up, and spoke to Perceval. And Perceval was still studying his own thoughts and did not hear. But Kay was fiery when he was not noticed, and let the flame come to his tongue with words, and called Perceval a dishonourable churl and a lying deaf dog, and said he was a landless man of no consequence and an unmannerly lout. Then, as the fire grew hotter the flame grew louder, and Kay was standing there in anger shouting and calling on God to strike obedience into the deaf and dumb.

The big lad was roused by the noise. He did not turn his head, but turned the haft of the big spear to Kay, swung it into the blue sky, and gave Kay the thump he had promised Owen would one day be ready; so that Kay rolled twenty feet through the snow and pitched on a rock, so that he broke his arm and the flat-bone of his shoulder. And his horse ran back to the king, Arthur, and Kay limped after, his fire quenched for then.

Gawain was there; and there was never a gentler knight. He said he would go and talk with the man on the hill. He came, and said; 'Sir, it would be agreeable to me if you would speak: if it would be agreeable to you to be heard.'

Then Perceval lifted his eyes from the snow and the raven and the spots of blood and the sky, and looked at Gawain.

'Is thou here yet?' he said.

'There were two before me,' said Gawain. 'I am the third.'

'Aye,' said Perceval. 'There was two fellows; and neither one of them would shift while I'd clouted them. One struck me without challenge, and the other shouted until I was stalled with the dirndum; and thou'll find either down the hill.'

'You will have been deep in a thought, perhaps?' said Gawain. 'It must have been a deep and noble and generous thought, that no man should have disturbed.'

'I were thinking on a lass,' said Perceval. 'And I thought I should go to her and court her and keep company. She is with the king, Arthur.'

'Your thought is a good one,' said Gawain. 'And when you think such a thought you should rebuke those that try to wake you from it; for God draws man and maid together, if they be free to join.'

'So now I go to the king's hall,' said Perceval.

'His hall is near here now,' said Gawain. 'And I have been sent to bring you down to it; and so indeed were the others.'

Then Perceval asked Gawain to speak to Kay, and tell him that there was something between them that must be endured. And Gawain told Perceval that the blow had been struck, and that Kay had his arm broken and the blade of his shoulder too.

'So,' said Perceval, 'then I have avenged that blow to the lass I thought long on as I stood here; and all is even between me and Kay and between Kay and the lass, and there is no more to fret over.'

Then they went down together to the king, Arthur; and Perceval came to the hall where the king laid, and was welcomed and honoured; and the girl was there that had not smiled more than once in two years; and she smiled again when she saw Perceval. And Kay did not strike her again, with either the broken or the whole arm. And they all had respect to Perceval, and made him a true knight of the company. And he was a great hero afterwards too, as it says in the books, and knew holy things; and to his mother that was a queen, he was always a big lad and no better and no worse for being a valiant knight in Arthur's hall.

The Battle of Roncesvalles

Retold by THOMAS BULFINCH

Roncesvalles is a village in northern Spain, a few miles from the Spanish frontier. Near it is the valley known as Valcarlos, where the battle was fought in which Roland died. In that year Charlemagne invaded Spain from France. He did not do so well as he had hoped in the fighting, and began to come back into France, hoping perhaps to return again the next year. But at Roncesvalles part of his army was cut off (you will see how in the story) and the battle followed. This is a story with its roots further back than the events it describes. The battle happened in 778; but the army that is described in stories and legends about Charlemagne (confusingly often called Charles for short without warning) is one that was in existence a hundred and fifty years before. For instance, the twelve paladins are probably a memory of twelve chiefs who tried the same invasion in 636. Whether they won or not, or if they did for how long, I do not know. The song of this battle and the hero Roland was sung at the battle of Hastings in 1066 (by the Normans: I don't know what Harold's men sang); and was well known for two hundred years after that, and is not forgotten now. This version is told by Thomas Bulfinch, a great collector and teller of old stories about heroic men. Roland in his time was prefect of the Breton marches, and was probably called Hruodland, which was turned to Roland gradually (and in Italy he was known as Orlando). The best language to read about Charlemagne and Roland in is French, and old French at that.

AFTER the expulsion of the Saracens from France, Charlemagne led his army into Spain, to punish Marsilius, the king of that country, for having sided with the African Saracens in the late war. Charlemagne succeeded in all his attempts and compelled Marsilius to submit, and pay tribute to France. Gan, or Ganelon, an old courtier of Charlemagne, and a deadly enemy of Orlando, had great influence over Charles;

and he was not without good qualities; he was brave and sagacious, but envious, false, and treacherous. Gan prevailed on Charles to send him as ambassador to Marsilius, to arrange the tribute. He embraced Orlando over and over again at taking leave, using such pains to seem loving and sincere, that his hypocrisy was manifest to every one but the old monarch. He fastened with equal tenderness on Oliver, who smiled contemptuously in his face, and thought to himself, 'You may make as many fair speeches as you choose, but you lie.' All the other paladins who were present thought the same, and they said as much to the Emperor, adding that Gan should on no account be sent ambassador to the Spaniards. But Charles was infatuated.

Gan was received with great honour by Marsilius. The king, attended by his lords, came fifteen miles out of Saragossa to meet him, and then conducted him into the city with acclamations. There was nothing for several days but balls, games, and exhibitions of chivalry, the ladies throwing flowers on the heads of the French knights, and the people shouting, 'France! Mountjoy and St Denis!'

After the ceremonies of the first reception the king and the ambassador began to understand one another. One day they sat together in a garden on the border of a fountain. The water was so clear and smooth it reflected every object around, and the spot was encircled with fruit-trees which quivered with the fresh air. As they sat and talked, as if without restraint, Gan, without looking the king in the face, was enabled to see the expression of his countenance in the water, and governed his speech accordingly. Marsilius was equally adroit, and watched the face of Gan while he addressed him. Marsilius began by lamenting, not as to the ambassador, but as to the friend, the injuries which Charles had done him by invading his dominions, charging him with wishing to take his kingdom from him and give it to Orlando; till at length he plainly uttered his belief that if that ambitious paladin were but dead, good men would get their rights.

Gan heaved a sigh, as if he was unwillingly compelled to allow the force of what the king said; but unable to contain himself long he lifted up his face, radiant with triumphant wickedness, and exclaimed: 'Every word you utter is truth; die he must, and die also must Oliver, who struck me that foul blow at court. Is it treachery to punish affronts like these? I have planned everything – I have settled everything already with their besotted master. Orlando will come to your borders – to Roncesvalles – for the purpose of receiving the tribute. Charles will await him at the foot of the mountains. Orlando will bring but a small band with him: you, when you meet him, will have secretly your whole army at your back. You surround him, and who receives tribute then?'

The new Judas had scarcely uttered these words when his exultation was interrupted by a change in the face of nature. The sky was suddenly overcast, there was thunder and lightning, a laurel was split in two from head to foot, and the Carob-tree under which Gan was sitting, which is said to be the species of tree on which Judas Iscariot hung himself, dropped one of its pods on his head.

Marsilius, as well as Gan, was appalled at this omen; but on assembling his soothsayers they came to the conclusion that the laurel-tree turned the omen against the Emperor, the successor of the Cæsars, though one of them renewed the consternation of Gan by saying that he did not understand the meaning of the tree of Judas, and intimating that perhaps the ambassador could explain it. Gan relieved his vexation by anger; the habit of wickedness prevailed over all other considerations; and the king prepared to march to Roncesvalles at the head of all his forces.

Gan wrote to Charlemagne to say how humbly and submissively Marsilius was coming to pay the tribute into the hands of Orlando, and how handsome it would be of the Emperor to meet him half-way, and so be ready to receive him after the payment at his camp. He added a brilliant account of the tribute, and the accompanying presents. The good Emperor wrote in turn to say how pleased he was with the ambassador's diligence, and that matters were arranged precisely as he wished. His court, however, had its suspicion still, though they little thought Gan's object in bringing Charles into the neighbourhood of Roncesvalles was to deliver him into the hand of Marsilius, after Orlando should have been destroyed by him.

Orlando, however, did as his lord and sovereign desired. He went to Roncesvalles, accompanied by a moderate train of warriors, not dreaming of the atrocity that awaited him. Gan, meanwhile, had hastened back to France, in order to show himself free and easy in the presence of Charles, and secure the success of his plot; while Marsilius, to make assurance doubly sure, brought into the passes of Roncesvalles no less than three armies, which were successively to fall on the paladin in case of the worst, and so extinguish him with numbers. He had also, by Gan's advice, brought heaps of wine and good cheer to be set before his victims in the first instance; 'for that,' said the traitor, 'will render the onset the more effective, the feasters being unarmed. One thing, however, I must not forget,' added he: 'my son Baldwin is sure to be with Orlando; you must take care of his life for my sake.'

'I give him this vesture off my own body,' said the king; 'let him wear it in the battle, and have no fear. My soldiers shall be directed not to touch him.'

Gan went away rejoicing to France. He embraced the sovereign and the court all round with the air of a man who had brought them nothing but blessings, and the old king wept for very tenderness and delight.

'Something is going on wrong, and looks very black,' thought Malagigi, the good wizard; 'Rinaldo is not here and it is indispensably necessary that he should be. I must find out where he is and Ricciardetto too, and send for them with all speed.'

Malagigi called up by his art a wise, terrible, and cruel

spirit, named Ashtaroth. 'Tell me, and tell me truly, of Rinaldo,' said Malagigi to the spirit. The demon looked hard at the paladin, and said nothing. His aspect was clouded and violent.

The enchanter, with an aspect still cloudier, bade Ashtaroth lay down that look, and made signs as if he would resort to angrier compulsion; and the devil, alarmed, loosened his tongue, and said, 'You have not told me what you desire to know of Rinaldo.'

'I desire to know what he has been doing, and where he is.'

'He has been conquering and baptising the world, east and west,' said the demon, 'and is now in Egypt with Ricciardetto.'

'And what has Gan been plotting with Marsilius?' inquired Malagigi; 'and what is to come of it?'

'I know not,' said the devil. 'I was not attending to Gan at the time, and we fallen spirits know not the future. All I discern is that by the signs and comets in the heavens something dreadful is about to happen – something very strange, treacherous, and bloody; and that Gan has a seat ready prepared for him in hell.'

'Within three days,' cried the enchanter, loudly, 'bring Rinaldo and Ricciardetto into the pass of Roncesvalles. Do it, and I hereby undertake to summon thee no more.'

'Suppose they will not trust themselves with me?' said the spirit.

'Enter Rinaldo's horse, and bring him, whether he trust thee or not.'

'It shall be done,' returned the demon.

There was an earthquake, and Ashtaroth disappeared.

Marsilius now made his first movement towards the destruction of Orlando, by sending before him his vassal, King Blanchardin, with his presents of wines and other luxuries. The temperate but courteous hero took them in good part, and distributed them as the traitor wished; and then Blanchardin, on pretence of going forward to salute Charlemagne, returned and put himself at the head of the second army, which was the post assigned him by his liege-lord. King Falseron, whose son Orlando had slain in battle, headed the first army, and King Balugante the third. Marsilius made a speech to them, in which he let them into his design, and concluded by recommending to their good will the son of his friend Gan, whom they would know by the vest he had sent him, and who was the only soul amongst the Christians they were to spare.

This son of Gan, meanwhile, and several of the paladins, who distrusted the misbelievers, and were anxious at all events to be with Orlando, had joined the hero in the fatal valley; so that the little Christian host, considering the tremendous valour of their lord and his friends, were not to be sold for nothing. Rinaldo, alas! the second thunderbolt of Christendom, was destined not to be there in time to meet the issue. The paladins in vain begged Orlando to be on his guard against treachery, and send for a more numerous body of men. The great heart of the Champion of the Faith was unwilling to harbour suspicion as long as he could help it. He refused to summon aid which might be superfluous; neither would he do anything but what his liege-lord had directed. And yet he could not wholly repress a misgiving. A shadow had fallen on his heart, great and cheerful as it was. The anticipations of his friends disturbed him, in spite of the face with which he met them. Perhaps by a certain foresight he felt his death approaching; but he felt bound not to encourage the impression. Besides, time pressed; the moment of the looked-for tribute was at hand, and little combinations of circumstances determine often the greatest events.

King Marsilius was to arrive early next day with the tribute, and Oliver, with the morning sun, rode forth to reconnoitre, and see if he could discover the peaceful pomp of the Spanish court in the distance. He rode up the nearest

height, and from the top of it beheld the first army of
Marsilius already forming in the passes. 'O devil Gan,' he
exclaimed, 'this then is the consummation of thy labours!'
Oliver put spurs to his horse, and galloped back down the
mountain to Orlando.

'Well,' cried the hero, 'what news?'

'Bad news,' said his cousin, 'such as you would not hear
of yesterday. Marsilius is here in arms, and all the world is
with him.'

The paladins pressed round Orlando, and entreated him to
sound his horn, in token that he needed help. His only
answer was to mount his horse, and ride up the mountain
with Sansonetto. As soon, however, as he cast forth his
eyes, and beheld what was round about him, he turned in
sorrow, and looked down into Roncesvalles, and said, 'O
miserable valley! the blood shed in thee this day will colour
thy name for ever.'

Orlando's little camp were furious against the Saracens.
They armed themselves with the greatest impatience. There
was nothing but lacing of helmets and mounting of horses,
while good Archbishop Turpin went from rank to rank
exhorting and encouraging the warriors of Christ. Orlando
and his captains withdrew for a moment to consultation. He
fairly groaned for sorrow, and at first had not a word to say,
so wretched he felt at having brought his people to die in
Roncesvalles. Then he said: 'If it had entered into my heart
to conceive the king of Spain to be such a villain, never would
you have seen this day. He has exchanged with me a thousand
courtesies and good words; and I thought that the worse
enemies we had been before the better friends we had become now. I fancied every human being capable of this kind
of virtue on a good opportunity, saving, indeed, such base-
hearted wretches as can never forgive their very forgivers; and
of these I did not suppose him to be one. Let us die, if die
we must, like honest and gallant men, so that it shall be said
of us it was only our bodies that died. The reason why I did

not sound the horn was partly because I thought it did not become us, and partly because our liege-lord could hardly save us, even if he heard it.' And with these words Orlando sprang to his horse, crying, 'Away, against the Saracens!' But he had no sooner turned his face when he wept bitterly, and said, 'O Holy Virgin, think not of me, the sinner Orlando, but have pity on these thy servants!'

And now with a mighty dust, and an infinite sound of horns and tambours, which came filling the valley, the first army of the infidels made its appearance, horses neighing, and a thousand pennons flying in the air. King Falseron led them on, saying to his officers: 'Let nobody dare to lay a finger on Orlando. He belongs to myself. The revenge of my son's death is mine. I will cut the man down that comes between us.'

'Now, friends,' said Orlando, 'every man for himself, and St Michael for us all! There is not one here that is not a perfect knight.' And he might well say it, for the flower of all France was these, except Rinaldo and Ricciardetto – every man a picked man, all friends and constant companions of Orlando.

So the captains of the little troop and of the great army sat looking at one another, and singling one another out as the latter came on, and then the knights put spear in rest, and ran for a while two and two in succession, one against the other.

Astolpho was the first to move. He ran against Arlotto of Soria, and thrust his antagonist's body out of the saddle, and his soul into the other world. Oliver encountered Malprimo, and, though he received a thrust which hurt him, sent his lance right through the heart of Malprimo.

Falseron was daunted at this blow. 'Truly,' thought he, 'this is a marvel.' Oliver did not press on among the Saracens, his wound was too painful; but Orlando now put himself and his whole band in motion, and you may guess what an uproar ensued. The sound of the rattling of blows and helmets was as if the forge of Vulcan had been thrown open. Falseron beheld

Orlando coming so furiously, that he thought him a Lucifer who had burst his chain, and was quite of another mind than when he purposed to have him all to himself. On the contrary, he recommended himself to his gods, and turned away, meaning to wait for a more auspicious season of revenge. But Orlando hailed him with a terrible voice, saying, 'O thou traitor! was this the end to which old quarrels were made up?' Then he dashed at Falseron with a fury so swift, and at the same time with a mastery of his lance so marvellous, that, though he plunged it in the man's body so as instantly to kill him, and then withdrew it, the body did not move in the saddle. The hero himself, as he rushed onwards, was fain to see the end of a stroke so perfect, and turning his horse back, touched the carcass with his sword, and it fell on the instant!

When the infidels beheld their leader dead, such fear fell upon them that they were for leaving the field to the paladins, but they were unable. Marsilius had drawn the rest of his forces round the valley like a net, so that their shoulders were turned in vain. Orlando rode into the thick of them, and wherever he went thunderbolts fell upon helmets. Oliver was again in the fray, with Walter and Baldwin, Avino and Avolio, while Archbishop Turpin had changed his crosier for a lance, and chased a new flock before him to the mountains.

Yet what could be done against foes without number? Marsilius constantly pours them in. The paladins are as units to thousands. Why tarry the horses of Rinaldo and Ricciardetto?

The horses did not tarry, but fate had been quicker than enchantment. Ashtaroth had presented himself to Rinaldo in Egypt, and, after telling his errand, he and Foul-mouth, his servant, entered the horses of Rinaldo and Ricciardetto, which began to neigh, and snort, and leap with the fiends within them, till off they flew through the air over the pyramids and across the desert, and reached Spain and the scene of action just as Marsilius brought up his third army. The two paladins

on their horses dropped right into the midst of the
Saracens, and began making such havoc among them that
Marsilius, who overlooked the fight from a mountain,
thought his soldiers had turned against one another.
Orlando beheld it, and guessed it could be no other than
his cousins, and pressed to meet them. Oliver coming up
at the same moment, the rapture of the whole party is not
to be expressed. After a few hasty words of explanation they
were forced to turn again upon the enemy, whose numbers
seemed perfectly without limit.

Orlando, making a bloody passage towards Marsilius,
struck a youth on the head, whose helmet was so strong as to

resist the blow, but at the same time flew off. Orlando prepared to strike a second blow, when the youth exclaimed, 'Hold! you loved my father; I am Bujaforte!' The paladin had never seen Bujaforte, but he saw the likeness to the good old man, his father, and he dropped his sword. 'O Bujaforte,' said he, 'I loved him indeed; but what does his son do here fighting against his friends?'

Bujaforte could not at once speak for weeping. At length he said: 'I am forced to be here by my lord and master, Marsilius; and I have made a show of fighting, but have not hurt a single Christian. Treachery is on every side of you. Baldwin himself has a vest given him by Marsilius, that everybody may know the son of his friend Gan, and do him no harm.'

'Put your helmet on again,' said Orlando, 'and behave just as you have done. Never will your father's friend be an enemy to the son.' The hero then turned in fury to look for Baldwin, who was hastening towards him at the moment, with friendliness in his looks.

''Tis strange,' said Baldwin, 'I have done my duty as well as I could, yet nobody will come against me. I have slain right and left, and cannot comprehend what it is that makes the stoutest infidels avoid me.'

'Take off your vest,' said Orlando, contemptuously, 'and you will soon discover the secret, if you wish to know it. Your father has sold us to Marsilius, all but his honourable son.'

'If my father,' said Baldwin, impetuously tearing off the vest, 'has been such a villain, and I escape dying, I will plunge this sword through his heart. But I am no traitor, Orlando, and you do me wrong to say it. Think not I can live with dishonour.'

Baldwin spurred off into flight, not waiting to hear another word from Orlando, who was very sorry for what he had said, for he perceived that the youth was in despair.

And now the fight raged beyond all it had done before;

twenty pagans went down for one paladin, but still the paladins fell. Sansonetto was beaten to earth by the club of Grandonio, Walter d'Amulion had his shoulder broken, Berlinghieri and Ottone were slain, and at last Astolpho fell, in revenge of whose death Orlando turned the spot where he died into a lake of Saracen blood. The luckless Bujaforte met Rinaldo, and before he could explain how he seemed to be fighting on the Saracen side received such a blow upon the head that he fell, unable to utter a word. Orlando, cutting his way to a spot where there was a great struggle and uproar, found the poor youth Baldwin, the son of Gan, with two spears in his breast. 'I am no traitor now,' said Baldwin, and those were the last words he said. Orlando was bitterly sorry to have been the cause of his death, and tears streamed from his eyes. At length down went Oliver himself. He had become blinded with his own blood, and smitten Orlando without knowing him. 'How now, cousin,' cried Orlando, 'have you too gone over to the enemy?' 'O my lord and master,' cried the other, 'I ask your pardon. I can see nothing; I am dying. Some traitor has stabbed me in the back. If you love me, lead my horse into the thick of them, so that I may not die unavenged.'

'I shall die myself before long,' said Orlando, 'out of very toil and grief; so we will go together.'

Orlando led his cousin's horse where the press was thickest, and dreadful was the strength of the dying man and his tired companion. They made a street through which they passed out of the battle, and Orlando led his cousin away to his tent, and said, 'Wait a little till I return, for I will go and sound the horn on the hill yonder.'

''Tis of no use,' said Oliver, 'my spirit is fast going and desires to be with its Lord and Saviour.'

He would have said more, but his words came from him imperfectly, like those of a man in a dream, and so he expired.

When Orlando saw him dead he felt as if he was alone on the earth, and he was quite willing to leave it, only he wished

that King Charles, at the foot of the mountains, should know
how the case stood before he went. So he took up the horn
and blew it three times, with such force that the blood burst
out of his nose and mouth. Turpin says that at the third blast
the horn broke in two.

In spite of all the noise of the battle, the sound of the horn
broke over it like a voice out of the other world. They say
that birds fell dead at it, and that the whole Saracen army
drew back in terror. Charlemagne was sitting in the midst of
his court when the sound reached him, and Gan was there.
The Emperor was the first to hear it.

'Do you hear that?' said he to his nobles. 'Did you hear the
horn as I heard it?'

Upon this they all listened, and Gan felt his heart misgive
him. The horn sounded a second time.

'What is the meaning of this?' said Charles.

'Orlando is hunting,' observed Gan, 'and the stag is killed.'

But when the horn sounded yet a third time, and the blast
was one of so dreadful a vehemence, everybody looked at the
other, and then they all looked at Gan in a fury. Charles rose
from his seat.

'This is no hunting of the stag,' said he. 'The sound goes
to my very heart. O Gan! O Gan! Not for thee do I blush,
but for myself. O foul and monstrous villain! Take him,
gentlemen, and keep him in close prison. Would to God I had
not lived to see this day!'

But it was no time for words. They put the traitor in
prison and then Charles, with all his court, took his way to
Roncesvalles, grieving and praying.

It was afternoon when the horn sounded, and half an hour
after it when the Emperor set out; and meantime Orlando
had returned to the fight that he might do his duty, however
hopeless, as long as he could sit his horse. At length he found
his end approaching, for toil and fever, and rode all alone to
a fountain where he had before quenched his thirst. His
horse was wearier than he, and no sooner had his master

alighted than the beast, kneeling down as if to take leave, and to say, 'I have brought you to a place of rest,' fell dead at his feet. Orlando cast water on him from the fountain, not wishing to believe him dead; but when he found it to no purpose, he grieved for him as if he had been a human being, and addressed him by name with tears, and asked forgiveness if he had ever done him wrong. They say that the horse, at these words, opened his eyes a little, and looked kindly at his master, and then stirred never more. They say also that Orlando, then summoning all his strength, smote a rock near him with his beautiful sword Durindana, thinking to shiver the steel in pieces, and so prevent its falling into the hands of the enemy, but though the rock split like a slate, and a great cleft remained ever after to astonish the eyes of pilgrims, the sword remained uninjured.

And now Rinaldo and Ricciardetto came up, with Turpin, having driven back the Saracens, and told Orlando that the battle was won. Then Orlando knelt before Turpin and begged remission of his sins, and Turpin gave him absolution. Orlando fixed his eyes on the hilt of his sword as on a crucifix, and embraced it, and he raised his eyes and appeared like a creature seraphical and transfigured, and bowing his head, he breathed out his pure soul.

And now King Charles and his nobles came up. The Emperor, at sight of the dead Orlando, threw himself, as if he had been a reckless youth, from his horse, and embraced and kissed the body, and said: 'I bless thee, Orlando; I bless thy whole life, and all that thou wast, and all that thou ever didst, and the father that begat thee; and I ask pardon of thee for believing those who brought thee to thine end. They shall have their reward, O thou beloved one! But indeed it is thou that livest, and I who am worse than dead.'

Horrible to the Emperor's eyes was the sight of the field of Roncesvalles. The Saracens indeed had fled, conquered; but all his paladins but two were left on it dead, and the whole valley looked like a great slaughterhouse, trampled into blood

and dirt, and reeking to the heat. Charles trembled to his
heart's core for wonder and agony. After gazing dumbly on
the place, he cursed it with a solemn curse, and wished that
never grass might grow in it again, nor seed of any kind,
neither within it nor on any of its mountains around, but the
anger of Heaven abide over it for ever.

Charles and his warriors went after the Saracens into Spain.
They took and fired Saragossa, and Marsilius was hung to the
carob-tree under which he had planned his villainy with
Gan; and Gan was hung and drawn and quartered in Roncesvalles, amidst the execrations of the country.

Völund the Smith

Retold by BARBARA LEONIE PICARD

*The gods are my favourite people among the Norse; but a god is not a hero;
so that I have to do without Thor and Loki and Baldur, and do without the
giants too, that were their enemies. This story is about a smith called Völund,
who is not such a stranger to England as it might seem. The Norsemen came
to England and they brought their names and their stories and their people
with them; and Völund the smith they brought with them too, and now he
is called Wayland Smith, and his forges stand here and there on the upland
roads that the Vikings and the Norsemen used to travel. He is said to be seen
at times shoeing horses, and doing other deeds. You may think it is a sad and
unnecessary thing that Völund should have been wounded so that he could
not walk well. But when that happens in the story it is really a matter of
things being put the other way about. What can a young man do, if he has an
injured or a deformed leg, or some disease has struck it? Nowadays it does
not matter much: but in the times of the Vikings there were only two trades,
sailing, and farming, and only whole men can fare well in either. So it was
natural that a crippled man would become a smith, who does not have to walk
far, whose strength is in his arms and his skill. So Völund would have been
crippled before he became a smith (and indeed, smiths in many lands were
often lame in some way, even in Greece).*

THREE brothers once lived on the shores of a lake, and their
names were Slagfid, Egill, and Völund. In their veins flowed a
certain measure of elf blood, which made them skilled and
wise above other mortal men. Slagfid and Egill were crafty
hunters, but Völund was not only mighty in the chase, he was
also a most cunning smith, and the work he wrought in gold
and silver and bronze was the finest ever seen.

One summer morning the three brothers came out from
their house and saw, sitting among the flowers at the edge of

the lake, three fair young maidens. One of them was twining herself a garland of blossoms; another was combing her hair, leaning over to look at her reflection in the water; while the third sang softly to herself. And beside each one of them lay a garment of white swan feathers.

The three young men went to them and greeted them and asked who they might be, and the maidens looked up and smiled. And the first, setting the garland on her head, answered, 'We are three Valkyrs, three of Father Odin's warrior-maidens from Valhall where the dead heroes dwell. As we flew above the clouds on the white wings of our swan-robes, we saw this lake and thought how it would be pleasant to while away an hour or two, sitting by the water.'

'How are you named?' asked Slagfid, gazing at her with admiration for her beauty.

'I am Hladgud,' she answered, and smiled at him.

'And how are you named?' asked Egill of the maiden who was combing her hair, and who seemed to him the loveliest sight in the world.

'I am Olrun,' she answered, and smiled at him.

In all this time Völund had not ceased to watch the maiden who had been singing, and now he asked her, 'And how are you named?'

'I am Hervor,' she answered, and smiled at him. And her voice when she spoke was no less sweet than it had been when she sang.

The three brothers sat down on the grass beside the Valkyrs.

'I would that you were here for longer than an hour or two,' said Slagfid.

'We may well remain till sunset, since we have found a welcome,' said Hladgud.

'What is a single day out of a lifetime?' asked Egill.

'You are right,' said Olrun. 'It is but a short time. We might well remain for longer.'

But Völund took Hervor's hand in his and said, 'Could you not remain for ever?'

And Hervor turned to the other maidens and asked, 'What say you, my sisters, shall we call this place our home?'

They considered a moment, then Hladgud said, 'I am a little weary of battles and the din and stress of war, and I should be glad of the peace by this lake.'

'And I,' said Olrun, 'am a little weary of the feasting and the combats in Valhall, and I should be glad of the quiet that is found in a small house.'

'And I,' whispered Hervor, 'am a little weary of being a warrior-maid, and I should be glad to be some good man's wife.'

So the three Valkyrs stayed with the three brothers in the house by the lake, laying their swan-garments by in a wooden chest. And Slagfid took Hladgud for his wife, and Egill took Olrun, while Völund wedded with the maiden of his choice, fair Hervor.

For seven years they could not have been happier, but in the eighth year a longing came on Hladgud and Olrun and Hervor to fly again through the air, and to hear once more the sounds of battle and rejoice in the deeds of warriors. And though at first they said nothing of this to each other, one day Hladgud spoke. As the three of them sat by the fire, their husbands being out in the forest hunting, she said, 'Is it not over-quiet here, my sisters, beside this silent lake?'

'In Valhall,' said Olrun, 'at this moment, the warriors test their strength in the courtyard with golden swords, and soon they will enter the hall to feast on boar's flesh and mead.' And she sighed.

'Sometimes,' said Hervor slowly, 'I long to wear once again my flashing helmet and ride through the sky at the Allfather's bidding. Do you not remember what it was like, my sisters?' And she brushed away a tear.

'A Valkyr should not weep,' said Olrun.

'A Valkyr need not weep,' said Hladgud, and she rose and
went to the wooden chest and took out the swan-garments
they had not looked upon for seven years. And the others
came to her, and as each took in her hands her own robe of
swan feathers, the longing grew too strong for her; and they
all three cast off the keys from their girdles and the bands
that bound their hair, and they slipped on their swan-
garments and stole from the house. And with a heavy beating
of wings, three white swans rose up into the air and flew across
the lake and away beyond the clouds.

When the three brothers returned from hunting, they
called out gaily to their wives to show them the game that
they had caught; but never a sound answered their glad
greeting.

'What can ail them?' asked Slagfid.

'Perhaps they jest with us and hide themselves,' said
Egill.

But Völund said nothing, for there was a strange wild
terror in his heart as he remembered the three white swan-
garments of the Valkyrs, and in silence he went to the chest
where they had been hidden, and found it open and empty,
and he stood there, still and staring. As though they came to
him in a dream or from a long way off, he heard his brothers'
voices calling, 'Hladgud, Olrun, Hervor, where are you?
Come and see the deer that we have killed.' And after a time
he said, 'They cannot hear you. They are gone.'

'Where are they gone?' asked Egill. 'Had they gone to
fetch water or kindling, we should have seen them as we
returned.'

'They are hidden somewhere,' laughed Slagfid. 'The
house is not so large, we shall find them soon enough.'

'They are gone,' repeated Völund, pointing at the empty
chest. 'Look.' And his brothers looked and saw, and they too
stood still and staring, unable to believe.

But at last Slagfid said, 'I am going out to seek my Hladgud.
If I travel fast enough, one day I shall overtake her.' And he

strapped on his snow-shoes and took his sword and his bow and set off to the south.

And Egill said, 'I am going out to seek my Olrun. If I wander far enough, one day I shall find her.' And he strapped on his snow-shoes and took his sword and his bow and set off to the east.

But Völund closed the chest softly and thought to himself, 'I will wait here for my Hervor, and maybe one day she will return to me.'

So he made up the fire and put to rights the empty house and waited.

And the idea came to him to make each day a golden ring for Hervor, that he might give them to her if she returned; so every morning he wrought and hammered the shining metal and made a ring for her, and each ring he strung on to a long cord which he hung from the low rafters of the hall to await her coming. And so the months passed until there were 700 rings, 700 golden rings shining in the firelight, strung from beam to beam across the end of the hall. But Hervor never came home to wear them.

Now there lived a king across the hills by the sea, Nidud the cruel, and he heard how, alone in a house beside a lake, dwelt one in whose veins ran the blood of the elves, and who was said to be the finest smith the world had ever seen. And he sent for his men and bade them go to Völund's house and bring back to him something which this smith had wrought, that he might see for himself how great his skill might be.

When they reached the house, Völund was in the forest hunting, but their leader pushed open the door which was always ajar against Hervor's return, and the men entered and saw the rings strung on a cord stretched from wall to wall of the hall. 'One of these rings shall we take back to our king,' said the leader; and he slipped a single ring off the cord and they left the house.

When Völund returned home he counted the rings, as was his daily custom, and found that one was missing.

'Perhaps it was Hervor who came and took it for herself,' he thought, and his heart beat fast with hope, as he set to work to make her yet another golden ring.

King Nidud looked at the ring his men had brought him, turning it this way and that in his hands; and at last he said, 'I have no smith in all my lands who can do such work as this. I would that Völund wrought for me alone and for no other man.'

Bodvild, his only daughter, stood close beside his chair and clasped her hands together. 'He must indeed have marvellous skill,' she whispered.

Nidud looked up at her and his hard face softened a little as he held out the ring to her. 'It is yours, my child,' he said. 'Wear it and take good care of it.'

With joy she put it on her finger, and with joy she kissed him. 'Dear father, thank you for such a truly wondrous gift.'

Nidud smiled. 'This Völund shall make other jewels for you and for all my house,' he said. He turned to his men and his voice was harsh again. 'Go, bind me this smith and bring him here, for he shall be my thrall.' And his men hurried from the hall, for they knew King Nidud gave no order twice.

But fair Bodvild gazed at the ring upon her finger and thought, 'Whatever other jewels my father may give me of the elf-smith's or any other man's making, this shall ever be my favourite among them all.'

So Nidud's men returned to the house by the lake, and in the moonlight they rode up to the door; and entering, they fell upon Völund even while he slept and bound him with strong ropes, and rode with him back to their master's halls, taking with them, for the king, Völund's sword which was of skilled and curious workmanship.

King Nidud looked at the sword and tested its strength and was well pleased. 'Is this your work?' he asked Völund.

'Whose else should it be, since your men stole it from my house?' answered Völund.

'And did you make the ring which my daughter wears?' asked Nidud.

'I made no ring for your daughter, nor for any other woman in your house,' replied Völund.

'Go, fetch me Bodvild's ring,' ordered Nidud, and some-one ran to do his bidding. But his wife, the queen, came her-self from the women's quarters, bearing the ring, for she wished to see with her own eyes what the smith was like who could work so skilfully.

When Völund saw the ring that he had made for Hervor and knew that another had worn it, he was angry. 'Give me back what's mine, you thief,' he demanded of the king, and would have fallen upon him, disarmed though he was, but that the king's men held him fast.

The proud queen looked him up and down and her eyes were cold. 'He is savage and unfriendly, this smith from beside the lake,' she said.

'I like your work well,' said King Nidud. 'Will you make for me and my house the things which we desire?'

'I will make nothing for you,' said Völund. 'Let me go. I am not your thrall.'

The king laughed; and the queen said quietly, 'You will do as we wish, Völund the smith.'

'I will make nothing for you,' repeated Völund, 'and I will be gone from your hated house as soon as I may.'

'It would be a pity if we were to lose you,' said King Nidud, 'and it must be prevented.'

'It were best,' said the queen, 'that we cut the sinews of his knee-joints and set him on the island of Saevarstad, lest he try to wander away from our lands.'

'That is well thought of,' said King Nidud, and he ordered it done. His two young sons came to look on and mock at the helpless Völund whose pleas and protests were in vain; but his daughter, the Princess Bodvild, sat spinning among her mother's maidens, waiting for her golden ring to be returned to her, and wondering what he was like who had fashioned it, and if he were unkempt and wild, with strange elfin eyes.

And when the sinews of his knee-joints had been cut, Völund might never run again, and he could only walk with pain. He was rowed in a boat to Saevarstad, a small island a little way out from the shore, where there was a house with a forge; and here he was left with gold and precious stones and tools to work them with. And every third day the king went himself over to the island with food and drink for Völund, and to fetch the things that the smith had wrought. And if he had made nothing, then no food or drink was left for him, so that he was forced to make for King Nidud and his family all the things which they desired: daggers for the two young princes, gold cups for the king, brooches and necklaces for Bodvild and the queen, and many things beside; whatever they demanded of him.

And with every hour that he remained prisoned on the island, toiling for him, Völund's hatred for the cruel king grew deeper, and he swore to be revenged one day, not only on the king, but on all his family; and while he hammered out the glowing metal and shaped the rich ornaments, he thought only of how he might escape. And at last he considered how with his elfin skill and knowledge he might fashion for himself a pair of wings, that since he could walk no distance, he might fly away. So with feathers taken from the birds upon the island and with scraps of metal taken from the king's hoard, he set himself to his task with a will; but sparing for it only a little time each day, so that the work he wrought for Nidud might not appear to be less than formerly.

While Völund longed for vengeance and worked upon his wings, in the king's house, Bodvild, with each new jewel that her father brought her from the island, wondered more and more what Völund could be like, and thought of him for a longer time each day.

And the two boys, King Nidud's sons, thought much on Völund also, and wished that more of the things he made might be theirs, than only those things which their father gave to them. And they talked together of it and wondered if they might not persuade Völund by promises or by threats to make them each a sword as fine as that which the king had stolen from him and which he ever wore at his belt, boasting of it to friends and strangers alike. And at last they made up their minds to row over to the island themselves, unknown to their father, and bid Völund fashion them two swords.

Saying no word to anyone, they rowed the little way to Saevarstad early one morning on a day when Völund's work on the making of his wings was well advanced. 'Make us two swords such as the one you made before, which our father wears,' they demanded. 'But tell no one of it.'

Völund looked at their greedy eyes and the hard lines of their young mouths, and the thought of his longed-for vengeance came into his mind. 'Did anyone see you come to the forge?' he asked.

'There was no one about to see us, smith.'

'Did you tell anyone that you had it in your minds to come to Saevarstad?'

The boys laughed. 'Do you take us for fools?' asked the elder. 'Whom should we tell that we wish you to use our father's bronze to make us weapons with? Our father, so that he may prevent us?'

'And if you should see fit to tell him yourself,' said the younger prince slowly, 'we shall say that you lie, and we shall bid our father devise fresh torments for you, so beware.'

'I shall not speak to your father of this,' said Völund quietly. 'I give you my word on that.'

'Then set to work and fashion us our swords with speed, and when seven nights are passed we shall return for them. And remember, not a word to the king,' said the elder prince.

'While we are here, brother,' said the younger, 'why do we not take with us as much as we can carry of our father's gold? It may be worth our keeping.'

'Show us where you have our father's gold,' they demanded of Völund; and he smiled and led them to a great chest which stood by the wall. 'In there is the gold,' he said. 'Open it and see, and take what you will of it, for it is not my right to prevent you.'

The princes raised the heavy lid of the chest and saw the gold all shining within, and cried out in their pleasure at the sight. And Völund backed a little way from them, to where an axe stood leaning up against a wooden pillar.

'Come, let us take the largest pieces,' said the elder brother; and they both knelt down on the floor and reached into the chest, running their hands through the glittering hoard.

And Völund took up the axe and moved softly behind them.

'This piece is mine,' said the younger boy. 'See, how large it is.'

'It is the largest of all,' said the elder, 'and it should be mine, since I have seen more years than you.'

'I found it first,' retorted his brother, 'and the best prize goes to him who has the sharpest eyes.'

'I saw it as soon as you, brother, but you cheated and snatched it from beneath my hands.'

'That is a lie,' said the younger boy; but his brother made to take the piece of gold from him.

Yet while they struggled for possession of their father's wealth, Völund raised the axe and struck. Twice he struck and twice the axe fell and the two boys died, still clutching at the gold. And Völund laughed a little to himself. 'They were fit sons of such a father,' he thought. 'And now is my vengeance begun.'

He drew up the boat from the beach and burnt it, so that no one might know that the princes had been to Saevarstad, and then he buried their bodies, all save the heads, beneath the sooty floor of the forge. But the two skulls he took and set in silver and made of them two drinking cups for Nidud the king, and with elfin runes he changed their eyes into gems for their mother the queen, while their teeth he set in a golden brooch for Bodvild their sister. And when King Nidud came again to the island, Völund smiled on him and gave him the gifts and King Nidud bore them away, little knowing what they were.

In the king's house it was thought that the two boys had gone hunting, and would be home after a few days had passed, so that at first no one grieved for them. And on the island Völund smiled grimly to himself, and worked long into the night, by firelight, fashioning his wings.

And when he had but a day's work left until they should be completed, Bodvild broke the golden ring that Völund had made for Hervor his wife, and she wept, for it was her favourite jewel. And though she longed that the break might be welded, she dared not tell her parents of it, for she feared that her mother might call her clumsy and her father might chide her for not keeping her jewel more carefully, and she thought, 'There is no one to whom I would dare to speak of this and ask his help, save only him who made the ring.' And because she longed to have her ring whole again that she might wear it as she was wont, and because she longed to see Völund for herself, she slipped early from her father's house, and rowed over to Saevarstad in a small, light boat. She knocked on the door of the smithy and Völund opened it and saw her standing there.

'You are welcome, princess,' he said, and stood aside to let her in.

Half afraid, she entered, her cloak clasped around her. 'You are alone?' he asked.

She nodded. 'Quite alone.' Then quickly she pleaded, 'You will not tell my father I was here, when he comes to you again?'

'She is alone, and no one knows her to be here,' thought Völund. 'Now will my vengeance be completed.' And he laughed in his heart. 'I shall not tell your father, princess,' he said, and closed the door. 'But why are you here, on Saevarstad?'

Shyly, she held out the ring to him. 'I have broken my ring. Will you mend it for me?'

When he saw again the ring that he had made for Hervor, he frowned and almost snatched it from her, so that she thought he was angry at her carelessness. 'I am sorry,' she said timidly. 'It was clumsy of me to break it, but I would not have had it broken for the world, for it is my favourite jewel.'

'You would have me mend it for you?' he asked.

'If you will.' She watched him as he looked closely at the break, and thought how he did not seem the wild elfin creature her mother had said him to be. She was glad that he was young, and though his looks had been spoilt by lines of suffering, he appeared to her eyes to be all that she had ever dreamt he might be. 'If only he would smile,' she thought, 'just smile once for me.'

Völund stared at the ring, but he did not see it, for he was thinking. 'The two boys are dead and here stands the maiden. A high price shall you pay, King Nidud, you and your queen, for your cruelty.' And he looked up, and from the triumph in his mind, he smiled at Bodvild; and because her eyes saw him with love as through a veil, she thought his smile was kindly and her heart rejoiced.

'Sit here and rest, while I mend the ring,' he said, and led her to a chair. He filled a cup with ale and brought it to her. 'Drink, princess,' he said. And she thanked him and took the cup.

He looked across to the pillar against which stood the axe with which he had killed her brothers. 'First,' he thought, 'must I weld the break in Hervor's ring, it must not be left broken longer.' And he went to heat the gold to mend it.

The ale was a strong man's drink, and the cup was large; but Bodvild thought that it would be discourteous in a guest to leave the cup unemptied, so she drank the ale, down

to the last drop. After, she put the cup carefully on the floor, and sat thinking for a little while; then, her heart made brave by the drink, she rose and walked a little unsteadily to where Völund worked on the ring beside the smithy fire. She stood there watching him until he was almost done, and then she spoke to him. 'Völund.'

He looked round, surprised to see her there. The flames shone on her golden hair and on her gentle eyes, and on her cheeks, flushed by the ale and by her own boldness. 'What do you want?' he asked.

'Only to tell you that I love you, Völund,' she said. 'And that it is a painful thought to me, the cruelty my father has shown to you.'

Völund smiled bitterly. 'You have drunk too much ale, and you do not know what you are saying.'

'I have drunk too much ale,' she said, 'but for all that I know what I am saying, and it is the truth. Yet if I had not drunk your ale, I would not have dared to say the truth to you.'

'Do you expect me to rejoice in such words from King Nidud's daughter?'

The tears shone in her eyes. 'I am not to blame for his cruelty,' she whispered.

Völund hardened his heart against her. 'That is nothing to me, princess.'

The tears trickled down her cheeks. 'Now that I have seen you, I shall always hate my father and my mother for what they have done to you,' she said. 'All my life I shall hate them. How could I do otherwise, loving you so well?'

And watching her, Völund realized that his vengeance was complete, for King Nidud and his queen had lost their daughter, more surely and more cruelly than though she lay dead beside her brothers beneath the floor of the forge; and for the first time he saw her as Bodvild, and not as Nidud's child.

She twisted her hands together. 'I shall never love another

man in all my days, yet if I may not have you for my husband, at least I may help you to escape from here.'

'I can leave this island without your help,' he said, but his voice was less harsh than it had been.

'Will you not take me with you?' she whispered. 'Even though I am my father's daughter, I would ever strive to make you a good wife.'

Völund took her hands in his and said gently, 'I had a wife named Hervor once, and she is the only woman I could ever love. I lost her, but I still hope that one day she may come back. Can you understand how it is with me?'

And after a time she took her hands from his and said, 'I understand well,' and tried to smile.

He took Hervor's ring from the anvil and held it out to her. 'Here is your ring,' he said. 'See, I have mended it for you.' And he slipped it on her finger.

When she went, he took her down to the shore, limping slowly to the water's edge, and helped her push the little boat out from the beach; and there they parted without a word.

A few hours' more work on his wings, and they were finished; and before the house on the island, Völund tested them and found that they would carry him. With great triumph in his heart, he flew across the little stretch of sea to the mainland, and through the air to Nidud's house. There he alighted on the highest point of the roof and called to King Nidud to come forth from his hall.

And Nidud came out and stood before his house and looked up at Völund, and his face was drawn with anxiety, for his sons had not yet come home, and never before had they been gone so long. 'How came you here, Völund?' he asked.

'On the wings that I made for myself. Think you not that I am a mighty smith?' And Völund laughed. 'Where is your daughter, King Nidud?'

'She sits by the fire and weeps, and will speak to no one,

and she looks on me and on the queen as though she hated us.'

'And where are your sons, King Nidud?' mocked Völund.

'They are hunting in the forest,' answered the king, 'and if they do not come home soon, I must go forth to seek them.'

Nidud's queen came out from the house, and her face was pale and wan as she looked up at the roof.

'If you would seek your sons, King Nidud,' said Völund, 'there is no need to go to the forest. Look under the floor of the forge that you built for me, and there you will find your sons. Their skulls I set in silver to grace your feasts, their eyes are gems for your queen, and your daughter wears their teeth in a brooch on her gown.'

Nidud gave a mighty cry, and the queen fell senseless to the ground. Völund laughed again. 'Now are you both paid for your cruelty,' he said, and spreading wide his wings, he rose into the air. The king called for his men to come with their bows; but when they came, Völund was too far away for their arrows to reach.

And never again in King Nidud's house was there peace or joy or love, but only hatred and despair. And always Völund flew onwards and onwards through the clouds, right across the world, ever seeking Hervor the Valkyr, his wife.

The Courtship of Lemminkäinen

Retold by WILLIAM MAYNE

The Kalevala is the Finnish national epic, or heroic poem. It was written in its present form in the early nineteenth century, by Elias Lönnrot, and he compiled it from ballads and folk-lore and stories that had been handed down by word of mouth from generation to generation. The story here is only a fragment of the whole, and is not even about the mightiest of the heroes, but about Lemminkäinen. Finland is all forest and water and rocks, and over the forest and water and rock there lies for half the year the snow of winter. In the far north the snow is almost everlasting, and there is always the yearly struggle between the wakening and warming spring and the frozen winter, and the retreat of the warmth in the autumn. In the colder regions of the world, where the living is hard, and where there are few people, the events of nature take on an air of importance that we have forgotten for the most part. Up in the high hills of the north the importance of the seasons is acknowledged, and honour is given to them. The forces of nature were worshipped before Christianity came to Finland, and the worship is not far away under the stories of the Kalevala; and even in this fragment the hero is really struggling with nature and good and bad, rather than with real things. But those aspects of the story are only there if you want to look for them. Otherwise it is just a story.

LEMMINKÄINEN was a great one for the girls, and why not? If it wasn't one he was after it was another, and if it wasn't another it was two or three more at a time. So of course he was a great goer-about too, up and down the country in his boat. The country itself was all islands, and Lemminkäinen was away up and down among the islands day in and day out, after the girls. His mother was wise, but not so wise she didn't think the world of him, and they lived on an island themselves; and she thought he would come to something and be a great fellow. But for all that she knew there were stronger men, and that Lemminkäinen would have to wait until he was in his own full strength before he did much more than eye the lasses in the islands. There were things he had not been told yet, and that he had to learn. But there is hard learning and easy learning, and who is to say which is longest remembered?

The songs he knew were love songs. But there were other songs in Kalevala, the land of Heroes, Finland. There were the songs of magic, the songs that gave mastery over beasts and people, and gave sight of the future to the wise and old. These were the songs he had yet to learn. So far in his life even his love songs were not magical enough, and did not bind the hearts and eyes of the girls for very long, up and down the islands.

Lemminkäinen did not know how ill-prepared he was for the adventures of his life. He was young and carefree, and did not rely on magic to go his way safely, but used his strength.

One day he came back from hunting, and told his mother he knew what he would do. 'I shall go to Pohjola,' he said, 'the Northern Lands, and see whether I can find a wife. I do not think I shall want to marry any girl from round here.'

'You will have met them all, and you will know,' said his mother. 'But for all that, you ought to stay longer at home. You are not ready yet to travel far away. Skill at hunting and fishing is not all. There are the secret arts that you have not learnt yet, the magic arts. And the men of the Northern Lands are very skilled at laying spells and putting singing magic to work against people from Kalevala. You would be snared yourself before you had gone very far into Pohjola. You are wiser than a fish or a squirrel, by so much; and the men of Pohjola are by so much again wiser than you.'

'Oh, that, and that, and that,' said Lemminkäinen. 'I have heard and I have heard; and still I am here. I will go, when I have had supper.'

'So you may,' said his mother. 'So you may,' and she did not believe him.

But after he had eaten his supper he did not stretch out down by the fire and sleep. Instead he brushed his hair, and made himself ready to go.

'Stay by the fire,' said his mother.

'No,' said Lemminkäinen.

'You will be killed,' said his mother. 'I have warned you.'

'Only once,' said Lemminkäinen. 'No more.'

'We shall see,' said his mother. 'You will be the death of me, too; and more than once, at that.'

But Lemminkäinen laughed at his mother. 'If anything happens to me,' he said, 'if anything happens, then, what shall I say? Then this brush that I have brushed my hair with for so long, this brush will bleed, and then you will know I am in danger.'

'Well then, off you go,' said his mother. 'And you will not get far, I daresay, before meeting some new girl, and then you will be back again.'

Lemminkäinen set out as he was, with his sword, and he rode northwards for day after day. The chief of Pohjola was Louhi, who was a woman, and the ruler of the land. Lemminkäinen came to her house at nightfall, and stopped outside in the snow. He had not told his mother exactly what he had intended when he set out. He meant to find and woo and marry the daughter of Louhi, who was famous for her beauty, and who had not taken anyone yet.

There was a feast going on in the house of Louhi, where there were minstrels and warriors, who could be overcome with the sword; and there were singers of magic, who could overcome him with songs.

He used the magic of a hunting song himself, and changed to a beetle, and came under the door of the house, and stood quietly. He had to take the whole company by surprise, or the magic would be laid on him first. So he walked to the middle

of the place, and then came back to his right size, and stood there with his sword, and shouted.

'Too much noise,' he shouted. 'There is too much noise. It is time you came to the end of your chanting and gave up, and let us hear the blessed silence that is also part of the song.'

Louhi herself came and stood in front of him, and all the singing stopped. That was what Lemminkäinen wanted. 'What do you want?' said Louhi. 'How did you get in here?'

'Wit and wisdom,' said Lemminkäinen. 'I only came to sing you a song. Listen.' And he began to sing. He sang one of the songs he knew, the song for moving a herd of animals to another place. And by the time he had finished all the men in the place had been moved away, except one. He was an old cowman, who had been in the corner, out of the way, because he was blind, and his name was Märkähattu.

'Hey,' he said, 'why have you left me? Why did you leave me here and not send me off with the other old men?'

Lemminkäinen had not troubled to send Märkähattu away, because he was so old and blind. 'Back to your corner,' he said. 'You will not trouble me, I know.' But Märkähattu walked off into the dark, which was as good as the day to him.

'Now, Louhi,' said Lemminkäinen, 'look sharp and bring that girl of yours out, the Maid of the North. I think I will marry her.'

'It is that, is it?' said Louhi. 'Well, you that come from the south, you must learn that she is not to be taken because you ask for her. There are things to be done first. For instance, you must first catch the Elk of Hiisi. And you must go on foot, with no horse to help you.'

Now this was as much as to say that he could not hope to marry the Maid of the North; because the Elk of Hiisi is the Elk of the Devil, that is to say, it is winter itself, and who can catch winter?

'I will do it,' said Lemminkäinen. 'And not be long about it either. You shall not trick me, Louhi.'

'That will be a beginning,' said Louhi.

So Lemminkäinen made himself skis, and he took his bow, and he set off to look for the Elk of Hiisi. And as he went he sang a song for all the world of snow to hear, and the song said that Hiisi himself was in danger, and the Elk would be caught and taken.

Hiisi heard the song, and got ready, as he does every year. He let loose the Elk, and it ran through the land, spoiling everything in its path, because where winter comes nothing is the same. The trees are touched and the ground is broken and the water hardened, and whole forests look as if they have died for ever; and small animals do die.

Lemminkäinen chased the Elk across the land. He had to

stop singing, even though he was a great hunter, because his breath and all his efforts were needed to catch the creature. His skis broke against boulders. His arrows fell from his quiver. Then, one day, in the middle of a dark forest, where the branches were too thick to let snow come down to the ground, and where it was dark and shadowy, he came upon the Elk, and tied it with a bark rope, and dragged it back with him to the house of Louhi.

'Here, Louhi,' he said. 'This is the animal you wanted.'

'It is indeed,' said Louhi.

'Then let me have your daughter,' said Lemminkäinen.

'There is another thing,' said Louhi, because she did not want to give her daughter up. 'There is the Horse of Hiisi. Bridle that and bring it, and then we shall see.'

'One is the same as another,' said Lemminkäinen, 'to a hunter like me. Now let me see your daughter only, and I will be on my way.'

So Louhi let him look at the face of her daughter, as she sat against the fire. Then Lemminkäinen went on his way to bridle and bring the Horse of Hiisi.

Now, the horse of Hiisi is the Sun. So it was the next time the sun rose that Lemminkäinen saw it, and that was a long time away, because the winter is one long night in Pohjola, far in the north.

But he saw it among the trees, lifting itself up, with its mane bright with flame, and its hoofs striking sparks of pure day from the rocks of the mountains.

Lemminkäinen had to get near to this burning creature without being burnt himself. So he remembered his hunters' magic songs, that he had brought with him from Kalevala; and he sang one, not a boasting song, like the one he had sung against the Elk, but a persuading song. It was a song asking for rain and hail and sleet and clouds, asking them to come and cover the fire of the Horse and cool it down, so that it could be bridled and brought to Louhi. When the Horse is burning it is the wildest creature made. When its fire is out it is the

tamest and the most tractable, and can be led and put to work.

Lemminkäinen sang his song. And the drops of rain began to fall. First they spat when they fell on the Horse. Then they began to raise steam from its burning coat. Then there was a fog about it, and then there was the hissing of a quenched fire, and the burning stopped, because the fire was out. Lemminkäinen stopped singing, ran to the Horse, put his bridle about its head, and led the Horse back to Louhi.

'Now,' he said, 'my time has come. Bring your daughter out to me.'

'It is a fine Horse, surely,' said Louhi. 'But it is a finer daughter that I have. There is one more thing that I need;

and that you must fetch for me. On the river of Tuonela there lives a white swan. Go and bring that swan to me dead, killed with one arrow only.'

'That is not much,' said Lemminkäinen; but he did not know that the white swan of Tuonela is Death herself. 'I shall do it,' he said. 'Let me speak to your daughter before I go.'

So Louhi let them exchange words; and Lemminkäinen went on his way.

He came to the river Tuonela, the river at the edge of the world, and he walked along its banks, until he came to a great waterfall, where the river went underground, and where the white swan lived, half under the earth and half in the twilight outside. But he was not alone. There was someone who had come this way not long before, and still stood by the river. It was the old cowman, Märkähattu, who had been jeered at by Lemminkäinen when he came first to Pohjola and Louhi's house. He saw Lemminkäinen coming, and sang a song that Lemminkäinen knew nothing about. He sang the song of the watersnake, and the watersnake came up out of the river, and bit Lemminkäinen, so that he lay dying by the river. Then Märkähattu came and threw the limp body into the river, and with his sword he hacked it to pieces as it floated there, and the pieces were taken by the swift water and under the ground.

But a jesting remark that Lemminkäinen had made when he left home came true. He had said, when he teased his old mother, that when his hairbrush bled, he would be in danger. And now blood came from his hairbrush. His mother saw it, and she wasted no time. She took her cloak and her shoes, and she walked straight out of the house and northwards, and came to Louhi's house.

'He comes and goes from here,' said Louhi. 'But he has gone as many times as he came, so I can say nothing of him. If he comes again, he will go again.'

So Lemminkäinen's mother went on again, until she came to the river, and there she found a belt that Lemminkäinen had worn, and an arm ornament. And that was all. And she saw that something had gone into the river.

She went down to the south again, to the great smith of Kalevala, and ordered from him a great rake to rake the waters of the river. When the rake was made she went back with it to the river Tuonela, and began to drag it through the water.

And she found the pieces of Lemminkäinen, where they still floated, and she brought them to the bank, and took them with her to Kalevala again, and when the winter was over she laid them in the sun by the beehives, and sang a magic song over them. And when she sang her song the bees came down on the poisoned flesh, and took out the venom of the snake, and laid honey and the scent of spring flowers on the wounds made by the sword, and the living wax from their own bodies they put against his heart and his hands and his eyes.

And in a little while he woke up, and stood, and spoke.

'Why, mother,' he said, 'what am I doing at home? You shouldn't have brought me, even if I did have a little difficulty. I'm off again to marry Louhi's daughter. So it's goodbye again.'

'Nay, lad,' said his mother, 'we've had enough of that; and I'm getting too old to come running after you again. You come on in the house and have your dinner, and you stop at home here. There's plenty of fresh lasses come on since you were away, so you needn't be stirring from this spot for a long time.'

'Well,' said Lemminkäinen, 'I don't think Louhi wanted me to have her, somehow. So I maybe will stop at home a bit.'

So he did, and there he has stayed.

Prince Marko and a Moorish Chieftain

Adapted by WILLIAM MAYNE

from a story by WOISLAV M. PETROVITCH

*In Serbia, where this story comes from, poor blind men are the chief singers;
or they were until Serbia became part of Yugoslavia, and perhaps blind
people have other things to do now. It is lucky that printing overlapped the
end of traditional story-telling, or there would be few treasuries of stories left
to be read and heard by the rest of the world. The great National hero of the
Serbians was Kralyevitch Marko (Royal Prince Marko). He was a
historical person too, like most of the best heroes, but actual history does not
say a lot about him. The one thing that is well known about him is a strange
one. During his lifetime, and before and after it too, the land of Serbia was
ruled by the Turks, and the Turks were very much hated and feared. But
Marko, though he was a Serbian, and though he was a Serbian hero, was
on the side of the Turks, and served the Sultan faithfully. It is an odd thing
that a man who served the country's cruel conqueror should be a hero of that
country too. The reason must be Marko's character. He was a true knight,
and never stooped to any petty act; and it is most likely that his loyalty to
the Sultan allowed him to ask favours for his own people; and it is almost
sure that his love of justice did much to lessen the sufferings of Serbia. Another
odd thing about Marko: his father, King Voukashin, was descended from
someone called Britanicus: perhaps an Englishman.*

A GREAT and powerful Moorish chieftain had built himself
a great stronghold and dwelling many storeys high, on a huge
rock by the sea. When it was complete he had glass put in the
windows (and glass was rare and costly in those days) and all
the rooms and halls hung with silk (and silk came in mere
handfuls from China in those days), and so the place was
furnished.

But he stood in all his new splendour and thought: 'Oh

castle, why have I built you? Why do I by myself need fine rugs and costly furniture, and why do I by myself have to stand behind glass to look out on the blue sea? I have no mother, no sisters, and I have not yet found a wife.' And when he had thought again he decided to go to the Sultan and demand his daughter in marriage. 'He must either give her to me, or meet me in single combat.'

So he sat down and wrote a most emphatic letter to the Sultan, saying: 'Sire, I have built a beautiful castle by the blue sea, but I have no wife to live in it with me. I must ask you, therefore, to bestow your lovely daughter on me. In fact, I demand it; because if you do not, then you must prepare to meet me face to face with swords.'

The letter reached the Sultan, and he read it through. Its meaning was plain; but he did not wish either to give his daughter to the Moor, or to meet him in single combat. So he looked instead for someone to fight for him, accept the challenge, and face the Moor. He promised gold for any man who would defeat the Moor. And many a brave man went out to fight; but not one ever came to Istanbul to claim the gold.

Gradually it came about that all the best fighting men of the country had lost their lives. But this was not the worst thing to happen. The Moor, at last, prepared himself in all his splendour, saddled his horse Bedevia with seven belts and a golden curb, with his tent to one side of the saddle and on the other his heaviest club. He jumped on to the horse, and rode straight for Istanbul, holding his sharpest lance at the ready.

When he reached the edge of the city he spread his tent, struck his lance well into the earth, and imposed on the people that lived nearby a daily tax, consisting of: one sheep, one batch of white loaves, one keg of pure brandy, two barrels of red wine, and a beautiful maiden. Each maiden, after being his servant for a day, he would sell in the market. This tax went on for three months, because no one could stop him. But this was not all.

One day the Moor went into Istanbul, riding wildly on horseback. He rode to the palace of the Sultan, and shouted out loudly: 'Sultan, give up your daughter at once.' But there was no answer, so he struck the walls of the palace so hard with his club that the precious glass in the windows broke and fell down into the street like rain.

The Sultan saw that the Moor might easily destroy the palace, and even the whole city. He was alarmed, because he knew that now the time had come for him to give up his daughter, or go out to fight and be himself killed; in which case the Moor would take his daughter at once. The Sultan had to swallow his pride, and ask for a fortnight's delay before presenting his daughter, to make the marriage feasts ready.

The Sultan's daughter shrieked and fainted when she heard what was to happen. 'Is it to marry a Moor that I have been brought up?' she said. 'Was my beauty to be kept for such a fellow? And is it true that a Moor shall kiss my face with his lips?'

That night, when at last he slept, the Sultan had a dream, in which a man told him that in the Empire of Serbia there was a city called Prilip, and that in the city lived the Royal Prince Marko, who was known among men as a truly great hero, though he was a Christian. The Sultan was a Muslim, and the Moor was a Barbarian.

So the next day the Sultan wrote an official letter to Prince Marko at Prilip, begging him to come at once to Istanbul and accept the challenge of the Moor, and saying that if he saved the Princess the Sultan would give him three horse-loads of gold.

When Marko read the letter he said to the messenger that brought it, 'Go back to your master, and tell him that I dare not come and fight the Moor, whom I have heard of. I am sure it is impossible for any man to win a battle with him, and what is impossible it is useless to attempt. If he broke my head from my body, what use would three, or thirty-three, loads of gold be to me?'

The messenger took the words back that Marko had uttered; and at once the Sultan offered Marko five loads of gold. But still he would not come, because treasure is no use to the dead, and he dared not fight. Even for the chivalrous sake of saving the Sultan's daughter he would not come out; because it was not possible for him to win, he said.

But the girl herself, when she heard of it, took a pen and wrote in her own hand, with her own blood, calling Marko her own brother in God, and asking him to be a true brother to her, and begging him not to let her be the wife of the Moor, and added the name of God and of Saint John, as well as offering seven loads of gold, and seven great presents, a golden plate decorated with a golden snake, with a gem in its mouth that gave forth light at all times, and a sabre set with gold, and in the hilt a sign so that the Executioner of Istanbul would not execute Marko without special permission from the Sultan.

Marko read the letter, and said to himself. 'Brother and sister in God we may be, and great presents she may offer; but it is still death to me to face that Moor. But since she has named God and Saint John, whom I fear more than I fear the Sultan, or the Executioner, or death itself, then I must go and fight the Moor, and die if need be.'

This time Marko sent back no answer to the letter. He went into his castle and put on his cloak and cap of wolves' skins. Next he girded on his sabre, took his sharpest lance, and went to the stables, where his horse Sharatz was. Now Sharatz was the famous horse of Marko, and piebald, and he had him for a hundred and sixty years. He fastened the seven belts under the saddle with his own hands, attached a leather bottle filled with red wine to one side of the saddle, and his war-club to the other.

He came quietly to Istanbul, and did not go to the Palace, but to a modest inn. Later in the day he led Sharatz out of the city to a lake, to let him drink. But Sharatz would not touch the water, but kept turning his head to the right and to the left. Then Marko noticed a maiden approaching him, covered with a long gold-embroidered veil. When she came to the edge of the water she bowed towards the water and said 'God bless you, green lake. God bless you, because you are to be my home for evermore. I am now to cast myself in you and die, because I would rather do that than be the wife of the Moor.'

Marko walked over to her, and said: 'What is your trouble? And why should you drown yourself?'

'Leave me in peace, ugly Christian,' said the princess. 'There is nothing you can do for me.' But she told him what was on her mind, and ended by saying how cruel was the attitude of Marko, who was the only man in the world who could help her.

'Do not curse me so,' said Marko, when he had heard. 'For I am Marko, and I have come to fight for you. But now go home, and say nothing to anyone, and I will fight when the time is right.'

And the princess told him that the next morning the Moor was coming to claim her.

'I shall be ready,' said Marko. Then he went back to the inn.

The next day he sat at his ease in the inn, drinking red wine. The innkeeper came along soon, and began to put up the shutters and send the people away. Marko asked him what he was doing, and the innkeeper said that the Moor was coming into the town for the princess, and had ordered all the shops and inns to close. But Marko did not let the innkeeper close the inn, saying that he wanted to sit at his ease and watch the Moor go by in all his wealth and splendour.

Then they began to hear him come, because the Moor had sent out for his own people and made up a great procession of them, to lead him to the wedding. He himself came on Bedevia, and when he came by the inn where Marko was he stopped, and said it was a wonder that one inn should not have obeyed the orders he had given to close. 'Either,' he said, 'there is no owner to the inn; or, if there is anybody inside he is a great fool; or perhaps he is a stranger who has not heard how terrible I am.' And he rode Bedevia up to the door to see who it was there.

It was Marko, drinking wine from a bowl that held twelve litres of liquid; and as always, each time he filled the bowl he drank only half, and the rest was for Sharatz.

The Moor came in, and was about to attack Marko when Sharatz barred his way, and kicked viciously at Bedevia.

Marko then got up, and put on his cloak and cap, but inside out, with the fur showing, so that he looked like a wolf, and came to fight the Moor.

Bedevia had been given such a kick by Sharatz that the Moor had gone back into the procession, and was walking along with it, for he was in no mood to linger, being on his way to his wedding. Marko leapt on to Sharatz, and began to fight his way along the procession, from the back towards the front, overcoming man after man, and scattering the rest in his progress.

The Moor wheeled round, and said: 'This is an unlucky day for you, stranger. Ill fortune is overtaking you faster than you are overtaking me. I imagine there is a demon in you that has sent you to attack me on this day, when you do not know what is going on; or else you are plainly mad. I shall leap over you and your horse seven times, and then I shall cut off your head.'

But Marko laughed. 'Not even once shall you spring over me,' he said. 'And never shall you strike off my head.'

But the Moor leapt at once, and would have carried out part of his promise of jumping over Marko if Sharatz had not been so well trained to fight on his own account. He leapt up at the same moment, and bit off Bedevia's right ear, so that blood ran down from the wound over her neck and chest.

And Marko and the Moor struggled in the street for four hours, without either giving way. But then the Moor saw

that Marko was overcoming him and Bedevia, so he turned and fled away, and Marko ran after him down the main street of Istanbul.

But Bedevia was so fast a mare that the Moor was getting away, and even Sharatz could not keep up with her. Marko remembered his great club, and he took it, and threw it, and even Bedevia could not go faster than that. The club struck the Moor between the shoulders, so that he fell from Bedevia, and Marko struck his head from his shoulders.

And then he turned back towards the palace, and found the princess waiting to greet him, and all the followers of the Moor fled away, now that their master was dead.

Marko took the princess to the Sultan, and threw the head

of the Moor at his feet. And then, after the tears of joy were dry again, he received the gold he had been promised, and the gifts the princess had offered, and went back to Prilip.

And the wild birds of the desert came and dwelt in the high castle of the Moor on the huge rock by the sea, and made their nests in his curtains, and no man ever lived there.

Horatius

LORD MACAULAY

Horatius was a hero of a plain sort, who lived in Roman times, at Rome. He was not one of the magic sort of heroes at all. He was a stout defender of his country, and perhaps we should not hear much about him if it were not for the verses of Lord Macaulay. I like to read stories in verse, because they carry themselves along well, and I think that the verse itself gives a sort of body to a story that is a test of endurance rather than an exciting tale with a sudden unexpected ending. The verse gives the whole thing a voice without making it tiresome, and is a very good way of getting along. Thirty-one of the verses have been left out in this version, where I, and others, have thought that nothing much was happening again and again. Take a leisure moment to read this story, which is in a version abridged by Janet Adam Smith.

> Lars Porsena of Clusium
>   By the Nine Gods he swore
> That the great house of Tarquin
>   Should suffer wrong no more.
> By the Nine Gods he swore it,
>   And named a trysting day,
> And bade his messengers ride forth,
> East and west and south and north,
>   To summon his array.
>
> East and west and south and north,
>   The messengers ride fast,
> And tower and town and cottage
>   Have heard the trumpet's blast.
> Shame on the false Etruscan
>   Who lingers in his home,
> When Porsena of Clusium
>   Is on the march for Rome.

The horsemen and the footmen
  Are pouring in amain
From many a stately market-place;
  From many a fruitful plain;
From many a lonely hamlet,
  Which, hid by beech and pine,
Like an eagle's nest hangs on the crest
  Of purple Apennine;

From lordly Volaterrae,
  Where scowls the far-famed hold
Piled by the hands of giants
  For godlike kings of old;
From sea-girt Populonia,
  Whose sentinels descry
Sardinia's snowy mountain-tops
  Fringing the southern sky.

And now hath every city
  Sent up her tale of men;
The foot are fourscore thousand,
The horse are thousands ten.
Before the gates of Sutrium
  Is met the great array.
A proud man was Lars Porsena
  Upon the trysting day.

But by the yellow Tiber
  Was tumult and affright;
From all the spacious champaign
  To Rome men took their flight.
A mile around the city,
  The throng stopped up the ways;
A fearful sight it was to see
  Through two long nights and days.

Now, from the rock Tarpeian,
  Could the wan burghers spy

The line of blazing villages
  Red in the midnight sky.
The Fathers of the City,
  They sat all night and day,
For every hour some horsemen came
  With tidings of dismay.

To eastward and to westward
  Have spread the Tuscan bands;
Nor house, nor fence, nor dovecote
  In Crustumerium stands.
Verbenna down to Ostia
  Hath wasted all the plain;
Astur hath stormed Janiculum,
  And the stout guards are slain.

I wis, in all the Senate,
  There was no heart so bold,
But sore it ached, and fast it beat,
  When that ill news was told.
Forthwith up rose the Consul,
  Up rose the Fathers all;
In haste they girded up their gowns,
  And hied them to the wall.

They held a council standing
  Before the River-Gate;
Short time was there, ye well may guess,
  For musing or debate.
Out spake the Consul roundly:
  'The bridge must straight go down;
For, since Janiculum is lost,
  Nought else can save the town.'

Just then a scout came flying,
  All wild with haste and fear:
'To arms! to arms! Sir Consul:
  Lars Porsena is here.'

On the low hills to westward
    The Consul fixed his eye,
And saw the swarthy storm of dust
    Rise fast along the sky.

And nearer fast and nearer
    Doth the red whirlwind come;
And louder still and still more loud,
    From underneath that rolling cloud,
Is heard the trumpet's war-note proud,
    The trampling and the hum.
And plainly and more plainly
    Now through the gloom appears,
Far to left and far to right,
In broken gleams of dark-blue light,
The long array of helmets bright,
    The long array of spears.

Fast by the royal standard,
    O'erlooking all the war,
Lars Porsena of Clusium
    Sat in his ivory car.
By the right wheel rode Mamilius,
    Prince of the Latian name;
And by the left false Sextus,
    That wrought the deed of shame.

But the Consul's brow was sad,
    And the Consul's speech was low,
And darkly looked he at the wall,
    And darkly at the foe.
'Their van will be upon us
    Before the bridge goes down;
And if they once may win the bridge,
    What hope to save the town?'

Then out spake brave Horatius,
    The Captain of the Gate:

'To every man upon this earth
　　Death cometh soon or late.
And how can man die better
　　Than facing fearful odds,
For the ashes of his fathers,
　　And the temples of his Gods.

Hew down the bridge, Sir Consul,
　　With all the speed ye may;
I, with two more to help me,
　　Will hold the foe in play.
In yon strait paths a thousand
　　May well be stopped by three.
Now who will stand on either hand,
　　And keep the bridge with me?'

Then out spake Spurius Lartius,
　　A Ramnian proud was he:
'Lo, I will stand at thy right hand,
　　And keep the bridge with thee.'
And out spake strong Herminius,
　　Of Titian blood was he:
'I will abide on thy left side,
　　And keep the bridge with thee.'

'Horatius,' quoth the Consul,
　　'As thou sayest, so let it be.'
And straight against that great array
　　Forth went the dauntless Three.
For Romans in Rome's quarrel
　　Spared neither land nor gold,
Nor son nor wife, nor limb nor life,
　　In the brave days of old.

Then none was for a party;
　　Then all were for the state;
Then the great man helped the poor,
　　And the poor man loved the great:

Then lands were fairly portioned;
   Then spoils were fairly sold;
The Romans were like brothers
   In the brave days of old.

Now while the Three were tightening
   Their harness on their backs,
The Consul was the foremost man
   To take in hand an axe:
And Fathers mixed with Commons
   Seized hatchet, bar, and crow,
And smote upon the planks above,
   And loosed the props below.

Meanwhile the Tuscan army,
   Right glorious to behold,
Came flashing back the noonday light,
Rank behind rank, like surges bright
   Of a broad sea of gold.
Four hundred trumpets sounded
   A peal of warlike glee,
As that great host, with measured tread,
And spears advanced, and ensigns spread,
Rolled slowly towards the bridge's head,
   Where stood the dauntless Three.

The Three stood calm and silent,
   And looked upon the foes,
And a great shout of laughter
   From all the vanguard rose:
And forth three chiefs came spurring
   Before that deep array;
To earth they sprang, their swords they drew,
And lifted high their shields, and flew
   To win the narrow way;

Aunus from green Tifernum,
   Lord of the Hill of Vines;
And Seius, whose eight hundred slaves
   Sicken in Ilva's mines;
And Picus, long to Clusium
   Vassal in peace and war,
Who led to fight his Umbrian powers
From that grey crag where, girt with towers,
The fortress of Nequinum lowers
   O'er the pale waves of Nar.

Stout Lartius hurled down Aunus
   Into the stream beneath:
Herminius struck at Seius,
   And clove him to the teeth:

At Picus brave Horatius
  Darted one fiery thrust;
And the proud Umbrian's gilded arms
  Clashed in the bloody dust.

(Several Etruscan heroes challenge the Three, but in their turn are laid low. Their fellow-warriors grow apprehensive.)

But all Etruria's noblest
  Felt their hearts sink to see
On the earth the bloody corpses,
  In the path the dauntless Three:
And, from the ghastly entrance
  Where those bold Romans stood,
All shrank, like boys who unaware,
Ranging the woods to start a hare,
Come to the mouth of the dark lair
Where, growling low, a fierce old bear
  Lies amidst bones and blood.

Was none who would be foremost
  To lead such dire attack:
But those behind cried 'Forward!'
  And those before cried 'Back!'
And backward now and forward
  Wavers the deep array;
And on the tossing sea of steel,
  To and fro the standards reel;
And the victorious trumpet-peal
  Dies fitfully away.

But meanwhile axe and lever
  Have manfully been plied;
And now the bridge hangs tottering
  Above the boiling tide.

'Come back, come back, Horatius!'
  Loud cried the Fathers all.
'Back, Lartius! back, Herminius!
  Back, ere the ruin fall!'

Back darted Spurius Lartius;
  Herminius darted back:
And, as they passed, beneath their feet
  They felt the timbers crack.
But, when they turned their faces,
  And on the farther shore
Saw brave Horatius stand alone,
  They would have crossed once more.

But with a crash like thunder
  Fell every loosened beam,
And, like a dam, the mighty wreck,
  Lay right athwart the stream:
And a long shout of triumph
  Rose from the walls of Rome,
As to the highest turret-tops
  Was splashed the yellow foam.

And, like a horse unbroken
  When first he feels the rein,
The furious river struggled hard,
  And tossed his tawny mane,
And burst the curb, and bounded,
  Rejoicing to be free,
And whirling down, in fierce career,
Battlement, and plank, and pier,
  Rushed headlong to the sea.

Alone stood brave Horatius,
  But constant still in mind;
Thrice thirty thousand foes before,
  And the broad flood behind.

'Down with him!' cried false Sextus,
  With a smile on his pale face.
'Now yield thee,' cried Lars Porsena,
  'Now yield thee to our grace.'

Round turned he, as not deigning
  Those craven ranks to see;
Nought spake he to Lars Porsena,
  To Sextus nought spake he;
But he saw on Palatinus
  The white porch of his home;
And he spake to the noble river
  That rolls by the towers of Rome.

'O Tiber! father Tiber!
  To whom the Romans pray,
A Roman's life, a Roman's arms,
  Take thou in charge this day!'
So he spake, and speaking sheathed
  The good sword by his side,
And with his harness on his back,
  Plunged headlong in the tide.

No sound of joy or sorrow
  Was heard from either bank;
But friends and foes in dumb surprise,
With parted lips and straining eyes,
  Stood gazing where he sank;
And when above the surges
  They saw his crest appear,
All Rome sent forth a rapturous cry
And even the ranks of Tuscany
  Could scarce forbear to cheer.

But fiercely ran the current,
  Swollen high by months of rain:
And fast his blood was flowing;
  And he was sore in pain,

And heavy with his armour,
   And spent with changing blows:
And oft they thought him sinking,
   But still again he rose.

'Curse on him!' quoth false Sextus;
   'Will not the villain drown?
But for this stay, ere close of day
   We should have sacked the town!'
'Heaven help him!' quoth Lars Porsena,
   'And bring him safe to shore;
For such a gallant feat of arms
   Was never seen before.'

And now he feels the bottom;
   Now on dry earth he stands;
Now round him throng the Fathers
   To press his gory hands;
And now with shouts and clapping,
   And noise of weeping loud,
He enters through the River-Gate,
   Borne by the joyous crowd.

They gave him of the corn-land,
   That was of public right,
As much as two strong oxen
   Could plough from morn till night;
And they made a molten image,
   And set it up on high,
And there it stands unto this day
   To witness if I lie.

And still his name sounds stirring
   Unto the men of Rome,
As the trumpet-blast that cries to them
   To charge the Volscian home;
And wives still pray to Juno
   For boys with hearts as bold
As his who kept the bridge so well
   In the brave days of old.

The Troubles at Hawaiki

Adapted by WILLIAM MAYNE

from *Polynesian Mythology* by SIR GEORGE GREY

The people of Europe were proud of their explorers, who in the sixteenth and seventeenth centuries began to sail round the world, voyaging across the Pacific for the first time. But they were not the first sailors there, nor the most remarkable. Before them were the Polynesians, whose voyages were just as extensive, made rather earlier, and in much more primitive conditions. The distance they travelled was as great, from the north of the Pacific (some say the Polynesians are from Eskimo stock) down as far as New Zealand; and their standard of navigation was high. Not for nothing does Sir Peter Buck (a Maori whose private name was Te Rangi Hiroa) call them the Vikings of the Pacific. They had the same urgent spirit and the same fighting qualities, and the same skill in sailing. They reached New Zealand in the year 925, rather before the Vikings sailed a similar distance in another sea and found America. History was different for the Polynesians though. They were far away from civilization and the arts of printing and music and the trade of inventions. Not until the sixteenth century did Europeans meet them, and then only the roughest sailors and whalers. Not until the eighteenth and nineteenth centuries did Europeans visit New Zealand. So that there is a body of stories, dating from not very long ago, and telling of the heroes of the Maoris and the Polynesians of the islands.

THERE was a dog that belonged to Houmai-tawhiti. Now this dog which was called Potaka-tawhiti, came into the house of Ueneku one time, and caused trouble. Either it walked where it should not have walked, or it touched what it should not have touched, or, more likely, it ate what it should not have eaten. So, when Ueneku and his brother Toi-te-huatahi saw the dog they killed it, which they were entitled to do, because of what it had done wrong. But after that Toi' took it and ate it.

The sons of Houmai, who were Tama-te-kapua and Whaka-turia, went looking for the dog. They went from village to village, until at last they came to the village of Toi-te-huatahi, and as they went they kept calling for Hou's dog, 'Potaka, Potaka, where are you?'

At last the dog heard, and he howled in the belly of Toi'. 'Aow,' he howled, 'aow.'

Then Tama-te-kapua and Whakaturia called the dog again, and again it howled, 'Aow.'

Toi' held his mouth shut as close as ever he could; but the dog still kept on howling in his inside. Then Toi' said: 'Oh, hush, hush. I thought I had hidden you in the big belly of Toi', and there you are, you cursed thing, still howling away.'

When Tama' and Whakaturia had come to see where the dog was, they said to Toi': 'Why did you not kill the dog, and then bring it back to us, so that we knew what had happened to it? We know you would not have killed it without good reason, and we should have remained friends. But now, cousin, now, you will hear more of this business.'

Then Tama' and Whakaturia went home, and began to plan their revenge. First they made stilts for Tama'. When the stilts were finished they went back to Toi's village, and came to the big poporo tree of Ueneku, and with the stilts Tama' was able to reach among the branches for the fruit, eat some himself, and throw some down to Whakaturia. They stayed eating the fruit for a good long time, during the night, and then they came home again.

They went on doing this every night, until at last Ueneku and his people found that the fruit of the poporo tree was nearly all gone, and they wondered where it had gone. They looked under the tree for signs and marks, and they found the marks of Tama's stilts.

That night they kept watch on the tree. While one party was coming to steal, the other was lying in wait to catch them.

They did not have to wait very long. When Tama' and his brother came, and while they were busy eating, those who were lying in wait rushed upon them and caught both of them.

Whakaturia was on the ground, of course, and they caught him. Tama' escaped, on his stilts, but they chased him, and caught him on the sea shore. As soon as they had firm hold of him, those who were holding on cried out: 'Some of you chop down his stilts with an axe, so that the fellow falls in the water.'

'Yes,' said the others. 'Let him fall in the water, let him fall in the sea.'

But Tama' called down to them: 'If you let me fall in the sea I shall not be hurt; but if you chop me down so that I fall on the land I shall be killed.'

The people who had captured him thought he spoke good sense, and they thought well of it, so they chopped him down on land, and down he came with a heavy fall. But in a moment he was on his feet, and off he went, like a bird escaping from a snare, and got safely away.

So the people of Toi's village went to see how Whakaturia was to be put to death. Some said: 'Kill him at once;' but others said: 'No, don't do that. Hang him up in the roof of Ueneku's hut, so that he will be stifled by the smoke and die that way.'

They all liked that idea, so they hung him in the roof of the house, and lit a fire, and began to dance. Their dancing, and the singing that went with it were not at all good, but shockingly bad. And they went on night after night dancing and singing and having a fire, until at last a report of what was going on came to the ears of his brother Tama' and their father.

Tama' heard that Whakaturia was hanging in the roof of Ueneku's house, and being stifled by the smoke. So he thought he would go and see whether he was still alive.

He went in the night, and arrived at the house, and climbed gently right up on top of the roof. He made a little hole in the

thatch, just over where his brother hung, and asked him in a whisper: 'Are you dead?'

Whakaturia whispered up to him, 'No, I'm still alive.'

Tama' whispered again: 'How do these people dance and sing? Do they do it well?'

'No,' whispered Whakaturia, 'they do it very badly. Even their friends who are watching jeer at them, and find fault all the time. I don't think dancing and singing could be done worse.'

Then Tama' said: 'Would it not be a good thing for you to say to them: 'I never saw anything so bad as the dancing and singing of these people'; and if they reply: 'Oh, perhaps you can dance and sing better than we do', you must answer that you can. Then, if they take you down and ask to see your dancing and hear your singing, you can answer that you are filthy from the soot, and that they had better give you a little oil, and let you dress your hair, and give you some feathers to ornament your head with. If they agree to all this, and you clean yourself and deck your hair and put on the feathers, and they then say that you are now ready to dance, tell them that you must first borrow Ueneku's red apron, and use his two-handed sword, and you will then be ready to show them how to dance. But I, Tama', will be outside the door of the house. And you will rush outside at the right moment, and I shall bolt the door and the window of the house, and we shall escape without danger.' And then Tama' stopped talking to his brother, and went down from the roof.

Then Whakaturia called down to Ueneku, and to all the people who were in the house: 'Oh, all you people who are dancing and singing there, listen to me.'

And down in the house they all said: 'Silence, silence, listen to what the fellow is saying who is hanging there. We thought he had been stifled by smoke, but no such thing; there he is, still alive.' So they kept quiet. 'Let's hear what you have to say, you in the roof there.'

Whakaturia said: 'I say that you don't know any good dances or songs, at least that I have heard, and I am getting bored with what you are doing so badly.'

And down below they shouted up to him: 'Are you and your tribe famous for your dancing and singing, then?'

'Their songs and dances are beautiful,' said Whakaturia.

'Can you do them, then?' said the people down below.

Ueneku said: 'Let him down.' And he was let down, and the people called out to him to start dancing.

'Make a bright fire,' said Whakaturia, 'and see how covered with soot I am.' And then he did all the things that Tama' had said to him, and was given oil, and dressed his hair, and took the feathers, and the red apron, and the two-handed sword.

Then he stood up to dance, and as he rose from his seat on the ground he looked bright and beautiful as the morning star appearing on the horizon, and as he flourished the sword his eyes flashed and glittered like the mother-of-pearl eyes in the head carved on the handle of the sword.

He danced down one side of the house, and reached the door. Then he turned and danced up the other side of the house, and reached the end opposite the door, and there he stood.

Then he said quietly to them: 'I am dying with heat. Just slide back the door and let it stand open a little way, so that I can feel the cool air.' So they slid the door back and left it open. Then they called on him to dance again.

Then Whakaturia rose up again to dance, and as he rose up in the house Tama' rose up outside, and stepped to the door, and sat down there, with two sticks in his hand, all ready to bolt up the sliding door and the window.

Then Whakaturia, as is the custom in the dance, turned round to his right hand, stuck out his tongue, and made hideous faces on that side; again he turned round to the left hand, and made hideous faces on that side. His eyes glared, and his sword and red apron looked splendid. Then he sprung about, and hardly seemed to stand for a moment at the end of the house before he leapt through the door, and was immediately beyond it.

Up sprang Tama', and bolted the door instantly. Back ran Whakaturia, to help his brother bolt up the window, and there they heard those inside cursing and swearing and chattering like a hold full of young parrots. Then they ran away.

A stranger, who was passing the house, pulled the bolts out of the door and window for them, and the crowd who had been shut in the house came pouring out.

The next morning Toi' and Ueneku were still vexed, because those who had taken the poporo fruit had escaped again. 'We should have killed them at once,' they said, 'and they would never have escaped in this way. And now in the days to come that fellow will be wanting revenge for having been hung in the roof of the house.'

So before long, to finish the matter, Toi' and Ueneku went to make war on Houmai-tawhiti and his sons. Some fell on either side of the battle; but at length a break was made in the wall of the town of Houmai-tawhiti, and a storming party of

Ueneku's troops broke down the fences and came into the town.

Houmai-tawhiti's people called out: 'Hou', Hou', here is the enemy pressing his way in.'

Hou' shouted in reply: 'Let them in, let them in, until they come to the door of my house, and I am waiting for them.'

And at the third time the storming party came to the door of Hou's house, and Hou' rose up with Tama' and Whakaturia and the struggle took place. And those of the enemy that were not slain were allowed to escape back to their own village, and those that stayed behind dead were taken and cooked and eaten.

But that was a great crime, done by Hou' and his house and his warriors, in eating the bodies of these people, because they were cousins after all, and only strangers should be eaten. So after that Hou' and his relations and his descendants were seized by fear and cowardice, and became fit for nothing, the whole tribe. Hou' died, and Whakaturia died, but Tama' and his children lived, and he determined to keep peace, so that his tribe might go on living. And the peace was long preserved.

The Death of Kwasind

from *The Song of Hiawatha*, by H. W. LONGFELLOW

Henry Longfellow was inspired by a German translation of the Finnish Kalevala to write Hiawatha. The Kalevala was written in a particular sort of verse, and so was the German translation that Longfellow got hold of. He took a great deal of matter from the Kalevala. The Song of Hiawatha owes a great deal to Lönnrot's poem, Kalevala, though it is about Red Indians rather than about Finland. But both races of people dwelt among woods and waterways, and were at the mercy of the wild weather and the seasons, so that to take from one setting and put in another was not to do harm. Hiawatha is more famous than the Kalevala, probably; but it may not be so well known as you think. Not many people now know more than three or four lines; but it is very entertaining to read. This piece from it is taken from two sections, The Friends of Hiawatha, and The Death of Kwasind. From the first section I took all that related to Kwasind, the strong man, and I added all The Death of Kwasind, joining them together so that I do not think you will see the mend.

> Dear, too, unto Hiawatha
> Was the very strong man, Kwasind,
> He the strongest of all mortals,
> He the mightiest among many;
> For his very strength he loved him,
> For his strength allied to goodness.
>
> Idle in his youth was Kwasind,
> Very listless, dull, and dreamy,
> Never played with other children,
> Never fished and never hunted,
> Not like other children was he;
> But they saw that much he fasted,
> Much his Manito entreated,
> Much besought his Guardian Spirit.

'Lazy Kwasind!' said his mother,
'In my work you never help me!
In the Summer you are roaming
Idly in the fields and forests;
In the Winter you are cowering
O'er the firebrands in the wigwam!
In the coldest days of Winter
I must break the ice for fishing;
With my nets you never help me!
At the door my nets are hanging,
Dripping, freezing with the water;
Go and wring them, Yenadizze!
Go and dry them in the sunshine!'

Slowly, from the ashes, Kwasind
Rose, but made no angry answer;
From the lodge went forth in silence,
Took the nets that hung together,
Dripping, freezing at the doorway,
Like a wisp of straw he wrung them,
Like a wisp of straw he broke them,
Could not wring them without breaking,
Such the strength was in his fingers.

'Lazy Kwasind!' said his father,
'In the hunt you never help me;
Every bow you touch is broken,
Snapped asunder every arrow;
Yet come with me to the forest,
You shall bring the hunting homeward.'

Down a narrow pass they wandered,
Where a brooklet led them onward,
Where the trail of deer and bison
Marked the soft mud on the margin,
Till they found all further passage
Shut against them, barred securely
By the trunks of trees uprooted,
Lying lengthwise, lying crosswise,

And forbidding further passage.
  '*We must go back,*' *said the old man,*
'*O'er these logs we cannot clamber;*
Not a woodchuck could get through them,
Not a squirrel clamber o'er them!'
And straightway his pipe he lighted,
And sat down to smoke and ponder.
But before his pipe was finished,
Lo! the path was cleared before him;
All the trunks had Kwasind lifted,
To the right hand, to the left hand,
Shot the pine-trees swift as arrows,
Hurled the cedars light as lances.

  '*Lazy Kwasind!*' *said the young men,*
As they sported in the meadow,
'*Why stand idly looking at us,*
Leaning on that rock behind you?
Come and wrestle with the others,
Let us pitch the quoit together!'

  Lazy Kwasind made no answer,
To their challenge made no answer,
Only rose, and, slowly turning,
Seized the huge rock in his fingers,
Tore it from its deep foundation,
Poised it in the air a moment,
Pitched it sheer into the river,
Sheer into the swift Pauwating,
Where it still is seen in Summer.

  Once as down that foaming river,
Down the rapids of Pauwating,
Kwasind sailed with his companions,
In the stream he saw a beaver,
Saw Ahmeek, the King of Beavers,
Struggling with the rushing currents,
Rising, sinking in the water.

  Without speaking, without pausing,

Kwasind leaped into the river,
Plunged beneath the bubbling surface,
Through the whirlpools chased the beaver,
Followed him among the islands,
Stayed so long beneath the water,
That his terrified companions
Cried, 'Alas! good-bye to Kwasind!
We shall never more see Kwasind!'

But he reappeared triumphant,
And upon his shining shoulders
Brought the beaver, dead and dripping,
Brought the King of all the Beavers.

    And these two, as I have told you,
Were the friends of Hiawatha,
Chibiabos, the musician,
And the very strong man, Kwasind.
Long they lived in peace together,
Spake with naked hearts together,
Pondering much and much contriving
How the tribes of men might prosper.
Far and wide among the nations
Spread the name and fame of Kwasind;
No man dared to strive with Kwasind,
No man could compete with Kwasind.
But the mischievous Puk-Wudjies,

They the envious Little People,
They the fairies and the pigmies,
Plotted and conspired against him.
  'If this hateful Kwasind,' said they,
'If this great, outrageous fellow
Goes on thus a little longer,
Tearing everything he touches,
Rending everything to pieces,
Filling all the world with wonder,
What becomes of the Puk-Wudjies?
Who will care for the Puk-Wudjies?
He will tread us down like mushrooms,
Drive us all into the water,
Give our bodies to be eaten
By the wicked Ne-ba-naw-baigs,
By the Spirits of the Water!'
  So the angry Little People
All conspired against the Strong Man,
All conspired to murder Kwasind,
Yes, to rid the world of Kwasind,
The audacious, overbearing,
Heartless, haughty, dangerous Kwasind.
  Now this wondrous strength of Kwasind
In his crown alone was seated;
In his crown, too, was his weakness,
There alone could he be wounded,
Nowhere else could weapon pierce him,
Nowhere else could weapon harm him.
  Even there the only weapon
That could wound him, that could slay him,
Was the seed-cone of the pine-tree,
Was the blue-cone of the fir-tree.
This was Kwasind's fatal secret,
Known to no man among mortals;
But the cunning Little People,
The Puk-Wudjies, knew the secret,

Knew the only way to kill him.
   So they gathered cones together,
Gathered seed-cones of the pine-tree,
Gathered blue-cones of the fir-tree,
In the woods by Taquamenaw,
Brought them to the river's margin,
Heaped them in great piles together,
Where the red rocks from the margin
Jutting overhang the river.
There they lay in wait for Kwasind,
The malicious Little People.
   'Twas an afternoon in Summer;
Very hot and still the air was,
Very smooth the gliding river,
Motionless the sleeping shadows:
Insects glistened in the sunshine,
Insects skated on the water,
Filled the drowsy air with buzzing,
With a far-resounding war-cry.
   Down the river came the Strong Man,
In his birch-canoe came Kwasind,
Floating slowly down the current
Of the sluggish Taquamenaw,
Very languid with the weather,
Very sleepy with the silence.
   From the overhanging branches,
From the tassels of the birch-trees,
Soft the Spirit of Sleep descended;
By his airy hosts surrounded,
His invisible attendants,
Came the Spirit of Sleep, Nepahwin;
Like the burnished Dush-kwo-ne-she,
Like a dragon-fly, he hovered
O'er the drowsy head of Kwasind.
   To his ear there came a murmur
As of waves upon a seashore,

As of far-off tumbling waters,
As of winds among the pine-trees;
And he felt upon his forehead
Blows of little airy war-clubs,
Wielded by the slumbrous legions
Of the Spirit of Sleep, Nepahwin,
As of some one breathing on him.

At the first blow of their war-clubs,
Fell a drowsiness on Kwasind;
At the second blow they smote him,
Motionless his paddle rested;
At the third, before his vision
Reeled the landscape into darkness,
Very sound asleep was Kwasind.

So he floated down the river,
Like a blind man seated upright,
Floated down the Taquamenaw,
Underneath the trembling birch-trees,
Underneath the wooded headlands,
Underneath the war encampment
Of the pigmies, the Puk-Wudjies.
There they stood, all armed and waiting,
Hurled the pine-cones down upon him,
Struck him on his brawny shoulders,
On his crown defenceless struck him.
'Death to Kwasind!' was the sudden
War-cry of the Little People.

And he sideways swayed and tumbled,
Sideways fell into the river,
Plunged beneath the sluggish water
Headlong as an otter plunges;
And the birch-canoe, abandoned,
Drifted empty down the river,
Bottom upward swerved and drifted:
Nothing more was seen of Kwasind.

But the memory of the Strong Man

Lingered long among the people,
And whenever through the forest
Raged and roared the wintry tempest,
And the branches, tossed and troubled,
Creaked and groaned and split asunder,
'Kwasind!' cried they; 'that is Kwasind!
He is gathering in his fire-wood!'

Tavadan

by CHARLES MOLIN

The great Indian civilizations of South America are all but forgotten. They perished as soon as the European set foot on the land. Indeed, the poor Indian of Central America had a prophecy in his mind, that a bearded saviour would come one day and all would be well. So that instead of fighting the bearded Spaniards when they rowed ashore, they welcomed them; and all was lost. But even if they had fought the battle would have been lost. Further South the forest is growing over the remains of the capital cities and the factories of the old times. Only here and there a handful of Indians keeps the stories going that have almost died out. This story is about Tavadan, who was the beginning hero of one race; a man, but with greater power than other men, and nowhere near a god. Perhaps, in those days, nature itself was different; or perhaps things have been added to the story, so that the hopes and fears of later men have been made part of the story. The story comes from a collection still being made by Charles Molin, who has allowed me to use this one, without telling me a great deal about it.

WHEN Tavadan came back from the seven labours and wonders which he had worked among men, he was full of the glory of the world. But all the same he remembered his parents, who still lived out in the hills in their cave, where they had first lived.

Tavadan left the places where the rest of mankind lived, the towns and villages, and left the road where they walked, and the rivers where they fished, and the fields where they worked, and came out among the wild grassy hills.

Towards the evening as he came to the valley where the cave was, he began to notice how silent the air was round him. No birds were singing. He thought at first no birds were left, but then he saw a small yellow bird fluttering in the bottom of a bush. So he caught in in his hands and said to it: 'Are you hurt, little friend?'

The bird, when it heard his voice, knew who he was and stopped fluttering. 'Ah, Tavadan, lord of men,' said the bird, 'we have all this week been preparing a cheerful home-coming for you.'

'It was not any cheerful noise that I heard,' said Tavadan. 'I heard nothing. I thought the birds had gone away, so I caught you in my hands to ask you why.'

'Oh, Tavadan,' said the bird. 'Oh Tavadan, I beg that you will put me on that bush again. Then I will say what I have to say, because if I say it when I am in your strong hands, it may be that you will forget about me and in your anger will crush all my life from me.'

Tavadan said: 'What is this sorrowful thing you have to tell me? What is there in the hills that would raise my anger? I have been all over the world of man, and seven times has my anger been raised, when I did the seven deeds, but never in the hills away from man have I ever sorrowed or been angered.'

'Then listen,' said the bird. 'But first put me out of your hand on to the bush.'

So Tavadan did as the bird asked, and when the bird had shaken its head, and spread its wings, 'for I am afraid that your anger will overtake me,' it said, 'before I have time to die, unless my wings are ready.'

'Speak on,' said Tavadan.

'I will say,' said the bird. 'It is this. The gods are jealous of you. Your mighty deeds among men have hurt their pride. Men no more talk about the gods, but about Tavadan the Great, Tavadan the Glorious, Tavadan the Conqueror. But among men they could do you no harm, but now, hearing that you were coming home, they have run ahead, and done a very ill thing.'

'The gods are my friends,' said Tavadan. 'Never have I forgotten to remember them in the morning and in the evening.'

'Alas,' said the bird, 'they are shallower than mortals, and no praise is enough for them. The morning and the evening are not enough, all day long they would have you listen for them.'

'It is known that they are not accountable,' said Tavadan. 'It may be that I have risen too early and slept too late, and that they were asleep when I called upon them.'

'They hate you,' said the bird.

'And what have they done?' said Tavadan.

'They came here last night,' said the bird, 'and took away the life of your father and your mother, and now their bodies lie cold in the cave.'

'It is a great cruelty to me,' said Tavadan, 'that they should let me rejoice with the people of man outside in the world, and take away from me the praise due from my father and my mother. But you need not fear, bird. I shall do you no harm, nor any harm to any living creature. But I will go up to the cave and bury my father and my mother, and make a great mourning for them.'

'We have been mourning all day long,' said the yellow bird. 'We have been mourning for your sadness, and fearing your rage on all the hills round about. Because we have heard of the things you have done all the wide world over. So we were very fearful.'

'Go in peace,' said Tavadan.

Then he made great strides across the hills to the cave, and when he had gone in and found his father and his mother laid on their beds, and as cold as the rock of the cave itself, he wept in sorrow. Then he went out into the hills again and made a grave. 'No creature shall ever see them again,' he said. 'Even the gods shall lose sight of them.'

To make the grave he heaped up the hills on either side and made a great pit, and when he had made the pit he laid in it branches of trees for a soft bed, and then he wrapped the bodies of his parents in the soft animal skins that they wore in life, and laid them together side by side, and built a house of rock over them over the rocky clay and then he turned aside a river that ran in the hills, and flooded the place where they were buried so that from that day to this there is a deep lake high in the hills, where no fish, no weed and no boat can ever be found.

'Now,' he said, 'we shall make all the world mourn in sadness.' And he went among the forests and bid the trees shed their leaves. He went among the mountains and had the mountains cast off their glad white mantles of snow. He went among the rivers and bid them weep. He called upon the clouds to veil all the land. He went among the people and told them to stop rejoicing. He went down to the sea and told it to draw back and bow its head. He went to the animals and told them to keep in their lairs. He went to the earth itself and told it to shake. He went even to the fire and told it to burn low, and to the Moon to tell her not to rise.

'Tomorrow be for all creatures and for the whole world a day of mourning,' he said.

So that night he slept for the last time in the cave of his father and his mother, and there was no fire and there was no noise, and there was no wind, and there was nothing but the mournful silence.

But there was one thing he had forgotten about. When he woke after his night's sleep, the Sun was rising beyond the mountains. Tavadan came to the mouth of the cave and looked at it, and called on it to stop, and not to come up that day. But the Sun was too far away to hear even Tavadan's voice, though the whole earth shook when he said it. The Sun went on rising.

'It shall not rise today,' said Tavadan. 'All creatures will be mourning all day. The Sun shall not rise.' So Tavadan leapt up, across the hills, across the mountains, until he came to the edge of the world. And there he stood in front of the Sun, looking full fully into the bright flames, and shouted to him not to rise.

The Sun looked down at Tavadan, and said: 'Oh mighty world, and mightier man, why do you speak?'

'Do not jeer at me,' said Tavadan. 'In this world today all things shall make a great mourning, and keep the day sacred in memory of my father and my mother, who were the first man and the first woman, and I was the first baby, and now the first among all men.'

'You speak loudly,' said the Sun. 'But I do not choose to rest. I have my work to do. It is ordained for me to go across the world once a day.'

'It is the saddest day in the world,' said Tavadan. 'Do not mock at me, oh Sun, though no man has ever spoken to you before, yet here am I, and I have ordered all other things to observe this sad time, and you shall observe it, too.'

But the Sun laughed and sent lightning up the sky, and went on rising.

'Stop,' shouted Tavadan. 'Stop!'

The Sun called back: 'I am too high to hear you, great baby that you are, howling on your earth.'

Tavadan grew very angry. He took two mountains and heaped them up together on the edge of the world, and climbed to the top of them. He put up his hand and caught the edge of the Sun and held it tight.

The Sun felt that something dragged, and pulled and pulled, thinking he would drag Tavadan up with him.

'We shall see who wins,' said the Sun.

'So we shall,' said Tavadan, and holding on to the top of the mountains with one hand and the edge of the Sun with the other, he had his hands among the flames that hang round like the fringe of a cloak.

The Sun pulled. Tavadan held. The Sun laughed once more, and sent lightning up the sky, and then pulled hard. But he stayed where he was, because Tavadan's hold was so firm.

The Sun grunted, and made another hard pull. This time he moved away from Tavadan, and when he looked down and would have laughed, he found that he had got away because his flaming fiery fringe had torn away. Tavadan had a handful of flames. He threw them down the sky, and they can sometimes be seen flaming across the night. Men call them comets.

Tavadan took another mountain and heaped it on the two he had already. He ran up to the top and placed his hands on the head of the Sun.

'Either go down, Sun, or I shall tear you down,' said Tavadan.

'It shall not be,' said the Sun, and blew flames all over Tavadan.

But Tavadan had been in fire before, and was not burnt. He put his hands on the Sun's shoulders and pushed down.

So there was that day the great fight between Tavadan and the Sun. In the morning they fought all along the edge of the world, with the Sun trying to rise above the mountains, and Tavadan trying to push him back where he had come. But as the morning went on, they went round to the North, keeping all the time below the mountains that are at the world's edge. All the morning not a single gleam of light came over the mountains.

'I shall push you under the world for the rest of the day,' said Tavadan. 'There you may burn and have your being, but upon the top of the earth you shall not shine today.'

'I shall shine where I wish,' said the Sun, but after that he said very little because he grew out of breath.

All day long in the earth there was nothing to be seen, except that to the North, now and then, a great spark would fly out where Tavadan had dashed the Sun against the mountains, and then there was the noise of great thundering, as the Sun roared in pain. But every time the Sun recovered his strength, and fought back against Tavadan. But he could not overcome the hero's strength.

Across the middle of the day they were at the Northern ice-pole, where Tavadan held the Sun so long upon the ice-mountain that it all melted and the Sun was diminished in strength because the ice came into his soul.

'Now I shall play ball with you,' said Tavadan, and for a

time he bounced the Sun up and down on the edge of the
world with the palm of his hand, like a child. But every time
the Sun touched the rocks of the world, it gathered more
strength, so that by the middle of the afternoon it was as
strong as it had been in the morning. When it was strong
Tavadan could only fight with one hand, because one had to
hold him down on to the earth. At this time, along the place
where they were there had been no mountains, but only the
deserts going flat across the edge of the world. Tavadan held
on to the desert so much that he drew mountains up from it
into the sky, and they are the highest mountains in the world.
But still the Sun stayed out of sight.

Then towards evening the Sun began to weary, and tried
to rise no more, but would sink down. Tavadan ran along the
tops of the mountains pushing it down so that it would be out
of the way quicker. And then they came to the gate of the
Sun, full two hours earlier than usual, although they had come
a long way round, because they had come round by the edge
of the world while the Sun usually went straight over the
top of the earth. The Sun was spent and out of breath.
Tavadan was tired, but still full of strength. The guardian
of the gate that leads under the world would not let the Sun
through.

'You are two hours early,' he said. 'I have no power to
open the gate early.'

'I beg for sanctuary,' said the Sun. 'Rescue me from this
violent man.'

'I can do nothing for you,' said the guardian of the gates
where the Sun goes in. 'You must wait two more hours.'

But the Sun begged for mercy, and Tavadan said to the
keeper of the gates, 'I am Tavadan. Let him in.'

So the guardian of the gates unlocked the doors, and the
Sun crept to the gates and lay beside them with all his fire
running from him like blood, and said to Tavadan: 'Oh
Tavadan, I beg for mercy, I plead with you to let me keep my
life, and to do my work all my days for the rest of time.'

'I will give you mercy,' said Tavadan. 'I have always given mercy when it has been asked for.'

'You shall always have my thanks,' said the Sun.

'There is but one thing,' said Tavadan. 'You must tell me that you are sorry you did not wish to mourn for my parents.'

'I am sorry,' said the Sun. 'I am sorry that I have been beaten, too, but I am sorry with my heart, as well as with my broken body, that I ever jeered at you, and would not do as you asked me.'

'It is well said, oh Sun,' said Tavadan. 'Is there anything I can do for you now?'

'Just push me through the gates,' said the Sun. 'I have no more strength left in me.'

So Tavadan helped him through the gates, and he went down to his own place under the earth for the night.

'And now,' said Tavadan, to the keeper of the gates, 'give me those keys,' and he took them and threw them out into space where they lie to this day because, he said: 'There shall be no more from this day on any hindering of the Sun. He has fought well, and has mourned my dead, and I say that in the future he shall go about at his ease.'

So from that day onwards, the Sun has gone about at his ease, and taken a shorter or a longer time as he wished to go across the earth. And as the year goes by he wanders to the North and the South looking over those old battle-grounds, and searching for Tavadan, not knowing that Tavadan, though a hero, has died and is no more.

Tavadan went into all the world and spoke to all the creatures and all the elements and all the parts of the earth, and said to them: 'Go your way tomorrow as you have always gone, the day of mourning is over, all things have mourned, the Sun and the Moon, the mountains, the rivers and the lakes and the mists and snows, and all creatures from the tiger to the humblest flea hopping upon the hedgehog, and all are free now to mourn no man any more. But all men, in remembering their own dead in time to come, shall remember the deaths of the first man and the first woman, and be in mourning themselves.'

That was the end of Tavadan's mourning, except next day when the Sun rose very late and very faint, Tavadan went up like a merciful hero, and helped the Sun across the sky, for a full week. The Sun was very stiff and lame and hot and sore, he could not manage his journey by himself. Tavadan went with him and tended his wounds and brought him across his course.

And that was Tavadan's fight with the Sun.

Thomas Berennikov

R. NISBET BAIN

Some might think this was merely a fairy tale. In a way it is; but it is one of those that seems to have something else behind it too. It has been my opinion for a long time that those fairy tales with a central character who appeals to me as a person rather than a figure made to do things, is probably a true story of some kind that has lost its way. Thomas Berennikov seems to me to be one of these people, and there seems to be something historical in the tale. I don't know what it is: it may be part of the history of a war the Russians had with the Chinese. It may not be the Chinese that were fighting (it may not even have been the Russians). It is of course an accident whether a hero survives into memory. Some of them will have died with all the witnesses to their deeds, so that there was no one left to sing about them. Some will have had poor singers to tell their story; some will have been heroes on the losing side, and their memory effaced for ever by the conqueror (though that cannot have happened often, because the hero story is the kind that is told by conquered people particularly). I believe, though I am not sure, that the name Thomas Berennikov means Simple Thomas, or something like it. Very well, he was a simple hero, not heard of except in this story. But a hero, I believe, for all that.

ONCE upon a time there lived in a village a miserably poor peasant called Thomas Berennikov. Thomas's tongue could wag right well, and in mother-wit he was no worse than his neighbours, but he was anything but handsome to look at, and for working in the fields he was not worth a button. One day he went into the field to plough. The work was heavy and his nag was a wretched hack, quite starved and scarce able to drag along the plough, so at last Tom quite gave way to woe, sat down on a little stone, and immediately whole swarms of blow-flies and gad-flies fell upon his poor creature from every quarter and stuck fast. Thomas seized a bundle of dry twigs and thwacked his horse about the back with all his might; the horse never stirred from the spot, and the blow-flies and gad-flies fell off him in swarms. Thomas began to count how many he had killed, eight gad-flies, and there was no numbering the slain of the other flies. And Thomas Berennikov smiled. 'That's something like!' said he, 'we've killed eight at a blow! And there's no counting the smaller fry! What a warrior I am, what a hero! I won't plough any more, I'll fight. I'll turn hero, and so seek my fortune!' And he took his crooked sickle from his shoulders, hung up his bast-basket by his girdle, placed in this basket his blunt scythe, and then he mounted his hack and wandered forth into the wide world.

He went on and on till he came to a post on which passing heroes had inscribed their names, and he wrote with chalk on this post, 'The hero Thomas Berennikov has passed by this way, who slew eight at one blow, and of the smaller fry without number.' This he wrote and went on further. He had only got a mile from this post when two stalwart young heroes came galloping up to it, read the inscription, and asked one another, 'What unheard-of hero is this? Whither has he gone? I never heard of his gallant steed, and there is no trace of his knightly deed!' They followed hard upon Thomas, overtook him, and were amazed at the sight of him. 'What sort of a horse is the fellow riding on?' cried they. 'Why, 'tis a mere hack! Then all this prowess cannot be in the horse, but in the hero himself.' And they both rode up to Thomas and said to him quite humbly and mildly, 'Peace be with thee, good man.' Thomas looked at them over his shoulder, and without moving his head, said, 'Who are you?' – 'Ilia Muromets and Alesha Popovich; we would fain be thy comrades.' – 'Well, maybe you'll do. Follow behind me, pray.'

They came to the realm of the neighbouring Tsar and went straight into his preserves; here they let their horses out to graze, and laid themselves down to rest beneath their tent. The neightbouring Tsar sent out against them a hundred horsemen of his guard, and bade them drive away the strangers from his preserves. Ilia Muromets and Alesha Popovich said to Thomas, 'Wilt thou go against them, or wilt thou send us?' – 'What, forsooth! do you think I'd soil my hands by going against such muck! No; go thou, Ilia Muromets, and show thy prowess.' So Ilia Muromets sat him on his heroic steed, charged the Tsar's horsemen, swooped down upon them like a bright falcon on a flock of doves, smote them, and cut them all down to the very last one. At this the Tsar was still more wroth, collected all of his host that was in the town, both horse and foot, and bade his captains drive the wandering strangers out of his preserves without ceremony. The Tsar's army advanced on the preserves, blew with their trumpets, and columns of dust arose in their path. Ilia Muromets and Alesha Popovich came to Thomas and said to him, 'Wilt thou go thyself against the foe, or wilt thou send one of us?' But Thomas, who was lying on his side, did not so much as turn him round, but said to the heroes, 'The idea of my coming to blows with this rabble! – the idea of my soiling my heroic hands with the like of them! No! Go thou, Alesha Popovich, and show them our style of fighting, and I'll look on and see if thy valour be of the right sort.' Alesha rushed like a whirl-wind upon the Tsar's host, his armour rattled like thunder, he waved his mace from afar, and shouted with a voice more piercing than the clang of clarions, 'I will slay and smash all of you without mercy!' He flew upon the host and began crushing it. The captains saw that every one took to his heels before him, and there was no way of stopping them, so they blew a retreat with the trumpets, retired towards the town, and came themselves with an apology to Alesha, and said: 'Tell us now, strong and potent hero, by what name we must call thee, and tell us thy father's name that we may honour it. What tribute must we give thee that thou mayst trouble us no more, and leave our realm in peace?' – ''Tis not to me you

must give tribute!' answered Alesha; 'I am but a subordinate.
I do what I am bidden by my elder brother, the famous hero
Thomas Berennikov. You must reckon with him. He will
spare you if he pleases, but if he does not please, he will level
your whole kingdom with the ground.' The Tsar heard these
words, and sent Tommy rich gifts and an honourable embassy of distinguished persons, and bade them say: 'We beg
the famous hero Thomas Berennikov to come and visit us, to
dwell in our royal court, and help us to war against the Khan
of China. If, O hero, thou dost succeed in smiting utterly the
countless Chinese host, then I will give thee my own daughter,
and after my death thou shalt have the whole realm.' But
Tommy put on a long face and said, 'What's that? Well, well,
I don't mind! I suppose I may as well consent to that.' Then
he mounted his hack, commanded his heroic younger brethren
to ride behind him, and went as a guest to the neighbouring
Tsar.

Tommy had not yet thoroughly succeeded in testing the
quality of the Tsar's kitchen, he had not yet thoroughly rested
from his labours, when there came a threatening embassy
from the Khan of China, demanding that the whole kingdom
should acknowledge him as its liege lord, and that the Tsar
should send him his only daughter. 'Tell your Khan,' replied
the Tsar, 'that I fear him no longer; I now have a firm sup-
port, a sure defence, the famous hero Thomas Berennikov,
who can slay eight at one blow of his sword, and of the lesser
fry without number. If life is not pleasant to your Khan and
your Chinese brethren, come to my empire, and you shall
have cause to remember Thomas Berennikov.' In two days a
countless Chinese host surrounded the city of the Tsar, and
the Chinese Khan sent to say, 'I have here an unconquerable
hero, the like of whom the world knows not; send out against
him thy Thomas. If thy champion prevails I'll submit and pay
thee a tribute from my whole Khanate; but if mine prevails,
thou must give me thy daughter, and pay me a tribute from
thy whole kingdom.' So now it was the turn of Thomas

Berennikov to show his prowess! And his heroic younger brothers, Ilia Muromets and Alesha Popovich, said to him: 'Mighty and potent hero, our elder brother, how wilt thou fight against this Chinaman without armour? Take our martial armour, choose the best of our heroic horses!' Thomas Berennikov answered thus: 'How then? Must I hide myself in armour from this shaven pate? Why, I could finish off this Chinaman with one hand quite easily! Why, you yourselves when you first saw me, said: "'Tis plain that we must not look at the horse but at the warrior"!' But Thomas thought to himself: 'I'm in a pretty pickle now! Well, let the Chinaman kill me if he likes – I'll not be put to shame over the business anyhow!' Then they brought him his hack: he mounted it in peasant style, struck it with his bunch of twigs, and went into the open plain at a gentle amble.

The Chinese Khan had armed his champion like a fortress; he clothed him in armour twelve puds (480 lbs.) in weight, taught him the use of every weapon, put in his hands a battle-axe eighty pounds in weight, and said to him just before he set out, 'Mark me, and recollect my words! When a Russian hero cannot prevail by force, he will overcome by cunning, so lest thou should get the worst of it, take care and do everything the Russian hero does.' So the champions went out against each other into the open field, and Thomas saw the Chinese hero advancing against him, as big as a mountain, with his head like a beer-cask, and covered with armour like a tortoise in its shell, so that he was scarcely able to move. So Tommy had recourse to artifice. He got off his horse and sat down on a stone and began to sharpen his scythe. The Chinese hero when he saw that, got off his horse immediately, fastened it to a tree, and began to whet his axe against a stone also. When Thomas had finished sharpening his scythe, he marched up to the Chinaman and said to him, 'We two are mighty and potent heroes, we have come out against each other in mortal combat; but before we pitch into each other we ought to show each other proper respect, and salute one

another after the custom of the country.' And he saluted the
Chinaman with a low, a very low bow. 'Oh, oh!' thought
the Chinaman, 'here's some piece of trickery, I know. I'll bow
yet lower.' And he bowed himself to the very ground. But
before he could raise himself up again in his heavy armour,
Thomas rushed at him, tickled him once or twice in the neck,
and so cut his throat through for him. Then he leaped upon
the heroic horse of the Chinaman, scrambled on the top of it
somehow, flourished his birch of twigs, tried to grasp the
reins, and quite forgot that the horse was tied to a tree. But

the good horse, as soon as he felt a rider on his back, tugged and pulled till he tore the tree up by the roots, and off he set at full gallop towards the Chinese host, dragging after him the big tree as if it had been a mere feather. Thomas Berennikov was terribly frightened, and began bawling, 'Help, help!' But the Chinese host feared him more than a snowstorm, and

it seemed to them as if he were crying to them, 'Run, run!' so they took to their heels without once looking back. But the heroic horse plunged into the midst of them, trampled them beneath its feet, and the huge tree-trunk scattered them in all directions. Wherever it plunged it left a wide road behind it.

The Chinese swore that they would never fight with Thomas again, and this resolution was lucky for Thomas. He returned to the town on his own hack, and they were all amazed at his strength, valour, and success. 'What dost thou require of me?' said the Tsar to Thomas, 'one half of my golden treasures and my daughter into the bargain, or one half of my glorious kingdom?' 'Well, I'll take half your kingdom if you like, but I wouldn't turn up my nose either at your daughter with half your golden treasure for a dowry. And look now, when I get married, don't forget to invite to the wedding my younger brothers, Ilia Muromets and Alesha Popovich!'

And Thomas married the thrice-lovely Tsarevna, and they celebrated the wedding so gloriously that the heads of all the guests ached for more than two weeks afterwards. I too was there, and I drank mead and ale and got rich gifts, and so my tale is told.

Acknowledgements

We wish to thank the following publishers who granted permission to reprint the following works:

'Horatius' from *The Faber Book of Children's Verse* edited by Janet Adam Smith, reprinted by permission of Faber & Faber Ltd.

'Völund the Smith' from *Tales of the Norse Gods and Heroes* by Barbara Leonie Picard, reprinted by permission of Oxford University Press Ltd.

A BOOK OF PRINCESSES

Selected by Sally Patrick Johnson

There is a time to read stories about people like yourself, and a time to read about people who are different. That is when you should read about princesses, for whether they are bullied or cherished, proud or simple, hardworking or spoilt, beautiful or long-nosed, they are always special.

In this book you will find every type of princess imaginable; some are nice, some are horrid, some pretty, some plain, and the stories about them have been told by such wonderful writers as Walter de la Mare, Hans Andersen, Oscar Wilde, Charles Dickens, A. A. Milne and George MacDonald.

It is a book for little girls, especially those who like to dream.

A BOOK OF PRINCES

Selected by Christopher Sinclair-Stevenson

Princes are special. No one can be so perfectly priggish or completely charming as a prince, so handsome, so generous, or even so blind to his own faults.

Take the princes in this book, for instance. Some are incurably romantic – like Prince Michael who toiled in shackles nearly seven years, merely to win the love of a heartless princess, or Prince Wish who could never believe there was anything wrong with his atrociously long nose. Princes can be dreadfully unlucky, or horribly sly, like Prince Pointedface, who tricked the kind fairy who gave him three wishes, or simply nice like the prince who saved little Daylight.

But whatever their characters, there is always *something* that makes a prince different from other people, especially when the stories are by writers like E. Nesbit, A. A. Milne, Charles Dickens, George MacDonald, or James Thurber.

HERO TALES FROM THE BRITISH ISLES

Barbara Leonie Picard

All the world worships a hero, and every part of Britain has its own legends about men of glorious valour and derring-do. In this collection you will find all the great names, from Cuchulain the champion warrior who, single-handed, defended Ulster against the whole army of Connaught, to Taliesin the Welsh boy who became a famous poet, prophet and magician.

There are plenty of rousing stories but the romantic ones are the most haunting. Deirdre's lament for her slain brothers, and the legend that Arthur and his knights lie sleeping in a cave until Britain needs them, have a poetry which will last forever.

THE WHITE DRAGON

Richard Garnett

There are really three white dragons in this story. One is a dragon used in an old mummers' play that is rediscovered in a junk yard, one is an ice yacht that Mark Rutter and his friends build and sail in the frozen fens of East Anglia, and one is a mysterious White Worme seen long ago on a hillside half an hour before sunset.

This is a bustling, cheerful story of a hard winter in the fens, and the doings of a group of lively teenagers in a small isolated community – skating, ice-sailing, telling ghost stories, amateur theatricals, and archaeology, and of course unravelling the secret of The White Worme. It will have a special appeal for anyone who likes realistic stories which explain properly how things are made and done.

For readers of eleven and over.

THE WEATHERMONGER

Peter Dickinson

A story about England in the future. But instead of everything being more civilized, something has gone wrong and we are back in the middle ages. Geoffrey and Sally find the origin of the magic, and because Sally is good at Oral Latin they destroy it and restore England to its modern self.

GINGER OVER THE WALL

Prudence Andrew

There were four boys in the gang, Toni Reynolds, Tiny Thomas, Andy Martin and Ginger Jenkins. Ginger was the leader, and they had a good headquarters in a pigeon loft, safe from Bert Hughes and his band of toughs. Then the pigeon loft burnt down, and Ginger's lot found another place, a cave in some waste ground near the canal. But a real adventure came along, a big and frightening one, far worse than being beaten up by Bert's gang; they got mixed up in a real crime and came near to disaster by hiding an innocent man from the police. Or was their friend Carlo as innocent as he said?

If you have enjoyed this book and would like to know about others which we publish, why not join the Puffin Club? Membership costs 10s. a year for readers living in the U.K. or the Republic of Ireland (15s. in European countries, 25s. elsewhere), and for this you will be sent the Club magazine Puffin Post four times a year and a smart badge and membership card. You will also be able to enter all the competitions. There is an application form overleaf.

APPLICATION FOR MEMBERSHIP OF THE PUFFIN CLUB

(Write clearly in block letters)

To: The Puffin Club Secretary,
Penguin Books Ltd,
Harmondsworth, Middlesex

I would like to join the Puffin Club. I enclose my membership fee for one year (see below) and would be glad if you would send me my badge and copy of *Puffin Post*.

Surname...

Christian name(s)..

Full Address...

....

....

Age.....................Date of Birth..............................

School (name and address).....................................

....

Where I buy my Puffins..

Signature (optional).........................Date...............

Note: Membership fees for readers living in:
The U.K. or the Republic of Ireland   10s.
European countries   15s.
Elsewhere   25s.